C0-AVZ-314

DISCARDED

PROJECT SELECTION UNDER UNCERTAINTY

Recent titles in the
INTERNATIONAL SERIES IN
OPERATIONS RESEARCH & MANAGEMENT SCIENCE
Frederick S. Hillier, Series Editor

* A list of the early publications in the series is at the end of the book *

PROJECT SELECTION
UNDER UNCERTAINTY
Dynamically Allocating Resources
to Maximize Value

STYLIANOS KAVADIAS
Dupree College of Management
Georgia Institute of Technology

CHRISTOPH H. LOCH
INSEAD

Kluwer Academic Publishers
Boston/Dordrecht/London

Distributors for North, Central and South America:
Kluwer Academic Publishers
101 Philip Drive
Assinippi Park
Norwell, Massachusetts 02061 USA
Telephone (781) 871-6600
Fax (781) 871-9045
E-Mail: kluwer@wkap.com

Distributors for all other countries:
Kluwer Academic Publishers Group
Post Office Box 322
3300 AH Dordrecht, THE NETHERLANDS
Telephone 31 786 576 000
Fax 31 786 576 254
E-mail: services@wkap.nl

 Electronic Services <http://www.wkap.nl>

Library of Congress Cataloging-in-Publication Data

A C.I.P. Catalogue record for this book is available from the Library of Congress.

PROJECT SELECTION UNDER UNCERTAINTY: Dynamically Allocating Resources to Maximize Value, by Stylianos Kavadias and Christoph H. Loch

ISBN 1-4020-7703-3

Copyright © 2004 by Kluwer Academic Publishers.

All rights reserved. No part of this work may be reproduced, stored in a retrieval system, or transmitted in any form or by any means, electronic, mechanical, photocopying, microfilming, recording, or otherwise, without the written permission from the Publisher, with the exception of any material supplied specifically for the purpose of being entered and executed on a computer system, for exclusive use by the purchaser of the work.

Permission for books published in Europe: permissions@wkap.nl
Permissions for books published in the United States of America: permissions@wkap.com

Printed on acid-free paper.

Printed in the United States of America.

Contents

List of Figures

Preface

This book is the result of a five-year research program on the selection of projects in New Product Development (NPD). Part of the material is based on the first author's Ph.D. thesis research.

Portfolio selection is an unsolved problem in the sense that no over-arching theory exists that addresses all relevant issues, which include strategy, differing mental models and social interactions of the players involved, in addition to the need to produce quantitative prioritization criteria. This book is rooted in the mathematical theory of resource-constrained optimization with the goal of maximizing quantitative returns – this is, in our view, the most comprehensive body of applicable theory. While we do not explicitly address multi-dimensional choice criteria (e.g., analytical hierarchy process), a limiting budget forces the multiple criteria back to optimization of a quantitative "composite goal".

At the same time, the book attempts to broaden the portfolio discussion in two ways. First, we offer simplified models appropriate for the NPD context, where the lack of precise data is typical. Second, we discuss not only the annual portfolio review, but also what should be done with ideas as they emerge, and how projects should be prioritized once they are funded and ongoing. We attempt to develop qualitative decision rules and robust principles that are more easily applicable in practice than complex mathematical programming models. We hope that the reader sees some value in this undertaking.

Atlanta and Fontainebleau, November 2003.

STYLIANOS (STELIOS) KAVADIAS

CHRISTOPH H. LOCH

Acknowledgments

We thank the editors, Gary Folven and Fred Hillier, for their patience and support in publishing this book. The INSEAD R&D fund supported the work of the first author, while Hewlett Packard hosted the second author while this book was put together. Also, we are grateful to the managers at our host company whose name we have disguised as "Gem-Stone," and to Staffan Tapper who accompanied this work with a critical eye.

Parts of our analysis have undergone the scrutiny of the academic review process, which helped us improve and extend our results, as well as clarify the message we want to convey. We thank the anonymous reviewers for providing us with their insightful comments and suggestions.

Finally, our research ideas benefited from useful discussions conducted with colleagues and friends. In particular, Laurens Debo (CMU), and Jose-Miguel Gaspar (ESSEC) provided sounding boards for ideas that later transformed into actual models.

Chapter 1

THE PORTFOLIO SELECTION PROBLEM

1.   Introduction

All companies that engage in new product development (NPD) face the important problem of selecting a project portfolio. A statement by the head of the R&D division of AstraZeneca, a big pharmaceutical company, illustrates that portfolio selection under budget constraints is difficult: "AstraZeneca has to rein in some of its most promising drug candidates due to the lack of resources to develop them simultaneously" (Financial Times, 16 October 2000). Choosing the NPD portfolio practically determines the firm's strategy for the medium-term future, and is the responsibility of the senior managers of the firm (Roussel *et al.* 1991, Cooper *et al.* 1998).

2.   Portfolio Selection: A Complex Task

Portfolio selection is concerned with resource allocation among an *ensemble* of projects – it is a critical feature that the projects must be viewed together rather than in isolation. The portfolio view is necessary because of project *interaction*, such as mutual enabling or incompatibility, or competition for the same scarce resources.

In particular, scarce resources often critically constrain the portfolio selection decision. It is common practice to pursue many projects in parallel in order to achieve broader product lines (mass customization) and higher market share (e.g., Reinertsen 1997; Ulrich and Eppinger 2003; Cusumano and Nobeoka 1998). In multi-project environments, scarce resources represent an important constraint, and resource allocation is a critical factor for success (Adler *et al.* 1995). Scarce resources may be budgets, equipment (analogous to bottleneck machines in production scheduling), specialists with unique areas of expertise (such as a critical department, e.g., a testing lab), or individuals (e.g., an engineer performing a highly specialized procedure).

In addition, the choice of the "right" new products or processes must consider consequences over multiple periods (e.g., years) and uncertain outcomes. The literature has repeatedly approached the issue from various angles, and management scientists have highlighted its inherently difficult nature. Major features of the selection problem's complexity are:

- High uncertainty along the dimensions of the project market value, and technical output. New product managers face risks related to the overall functionality of the product (technical risk) and to the adoption of the product from the end customers (market risk).

- The dynamic nature of the decision (i.e., R&D managers need to allocate specific amounts of resources every year). Therefore, R&D management needs to take into account future potential or risk when allocating resources to a promising idea. However, it is often difficult to quantify the potential of promising ideas, making the allocation of resources (based on intangible rewards) difficult.

- Scarce resources inhibit timely project progress. Apart from a general constraint due to the R&D budget, project managers sometimes have to "queue" for access to specialized resources (e.g., testing labs, see Adler *et al.* 1995).

- Interactions among projects. Companies often develop multiple products and services in closely related market segments. Hence, the new products that they develop exhibit synergies or incompatibilities in their technical aspects. Similarly, on the market side, products substitute or complement one another.

A graphical illustration of the difficulty of the portfolio selection problem is depicted in Figure 1.1. A number of product lines or projects has to be funded by a resource budget in every period. At an operational level, the budget has to be shared among on-going projects competing for access to it, while at a strategic business unit (SBU) level the R&D manager has to decide how much to invest in the different product lines of the SBU. The projects, or the product lines, are targeted at different, but not necessarily independent, markets, producing uncertain payoffs over time. An additional complicating feature is the possibility of technical synergies and/or incompatibilities between projects, which has to be accounted for when composing the optimal portfolio.

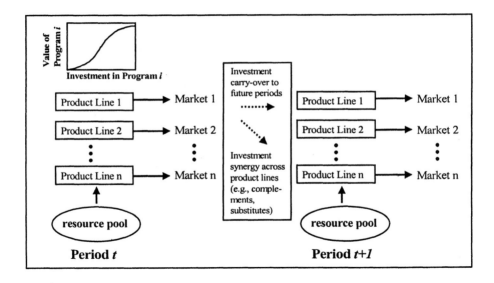

Figure 1.1. The Dynamic Portfolio Selection Problem

Because of this complexity, decision-theoretic models have not found widespread use in practice (e.g., Souder 1973; Schmidt and Freeland 1992; Loch *et al.* 2001). Managers tend to complement their routine financial project evaluations with *ad hoc* tools, in particular combinations of risk-return matrices, and portfolio balances over "strategic" market segments and over multiple period cash flows (Wheelwright and Clark 1992a; Cooper *et al.* 1998). Some representative, often used,[1] managerial tools are depicted in Figure 1.2. In **scoring models** (top of the Figure), various projects are ranked with respect to a weighted average of normalized performance on multiple criteria defined by management. The n best projects, according to their overall score, "make it" to the portfolio. The extent of (manufacturing or sales) process change versus the extent of product change balance (middle right of Figure 1.2) was introduced by Wheelwright and Clark 1992a. Their idea is that a large change in either of these two dimensions increases risk, which must be balanced in order to achieve better "planning, staffing, and guiding of individual projects" (Wheelwright and Clark 1992a). Finally, the risk-return matrix (bottom left of Figure 1.2) proposes a balance between the overall risk and the return of the portfolio. The "efficient frontier" characterizes the best returns that are being obtained at given risk levels. This tool is widely used in practice (see, e.g., Cooper *et al.* 1998).

The problem with these tools is that they generate only ad hoc rules of thumb: although they help management to "think through" a problem, they lack a theoretical or empirical basis for the resulting recommendations.

A relatively new approach is based on the idea that generic criteria, such as risk, return or any type of score, are not sufficient. Rather, the

---

[1]See Taggart and Blaxter 1992; Braunstein and Salsamendi 1994; Foster 1996; Groenveld 1997; Stillman 1997; Comstock and Sjolseth 1999; Tritle *et al.* 2000).

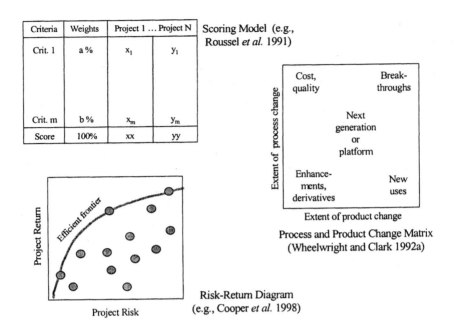

Figure 1.2.   Qualitative Portfolio Selection Tools

NPD activities should be explicitly linked to the goals of the business strategy (e.g., Kaplan and Norton 1996; Wheelwright and Clark 1992b; Comstock and Sjolseth 1999). The R&D strategy must be "cascaded" down to the individual activities instead of allocating a given budget according to (generic or customized) scores. We give an example of this approach in Section 4 of Chapter 2.

3.   Research Questions and Overview of this Book

This book addresses the question: *How to use financial return estimates in order to select NPD activities, at the aggregate level (programs) and the operational level (projects), and prioritize them as they unfold?*

While we do not address qualitative considerations at the highest strategic level, we *do* attempt to account for the data unavailability and inaccuracy that characterize real world project selection, seeking robust managerial rules that are relevant for practicing managers.

After reviewing the relevant literature in the fields of Operations Management, Operations Research (OR), Economics, and Finance in Chapter 2, we address the resource allocation problem as a *set of related problems*.

First, we discuss classic portfolio decisions (evaluating an ensemble of projects together). We begin with the aggregate allocation of resources to product lines at the strategic business unit (SBU) level (Chapter 3), and then we present an application of this theory to individual projects in practice, using a simplified approach that acknowledges limitations in data availability (Chapter 4). Subsequently, we go beyond the classic portfolio problem by acknowledging two limitations that practicing managers have to deal with, and that are not widely addressed in academic research: (A) periodic portfolio reviews do not fully address the allocation question because project ideas or opportunities may "arrive" *one-by-one* and require quick admission decisions, without the possibility of re-examining the entire portfolio (the decision may simply specify whether a project is "frozen" until the next portfolio review). Chapter 5 examines the "admission policy" question. (B) Even when an organization has a "perfect" portfolio, this does not resolve issues of *operational prioritization* – once the projects in the portfolio are funded and under way, they will compete for preferential access to scarce resources in execution (literally, project managers "yell and scream" over access). Operational priority is not settled by aggregate funding and strategic priority decisions. Chapter 6 discusses the operational prioritization among **ongoing** projects.

This book addresses the portfolio problem in a wider sense than is usually the case. The term "Portfolio Management", as it is normally used in Operations Management, does not address the entire set of problems that managers have to grapple with. By focusing on a larger part of the set than usual, we attempt to make a contribution. In more detail, the chapter contents are as follows.

In Chapter 3, the unit of analysis is the R&D *program*, or the collection of projects supporting innovation of one product line. The research question is: *How should SBU management allocate the R&D budget of its product development organization across its various product lines, considering their returns on investment, and uncertain payoffs?* We develop a stylized model of portfolio choice, which includes multiple periods, and multiple product lines that interact through a common resource pool as well as through complementarities, uncertainty, and management risk aversion. The key insight is that program allocations are continuously variable decision variables, not yes or no decisions. Therefore, we can derive results based on marginal returns rather than via combinatorial optimization.

Our results make two contributions: on the theoretical side, we offer one of the first comprehensive models of strategic NPD resource allocation with closed-form solutions. On the managerial side, the solution characteristics can be translated into qualitative managerial guidelines. The model shows that the interactions of the influence parameters are subtle, partly non-intuitive, and complex. However, many of the parameters can only be roughly estimated. Thus, the resulting complexity cannot usually be captured by numerical sensitivity analysis, not to speak of ad hoc rules without a theoretical basis. Therefore, the qualitative rules based on a rigorous model may better help managers to check their rules of thumb and to understand the directional impact of changes in technology or markets.

In Chapter 4, we consider the product selection process in a real application setting. The theme is the prioritization of project activities in the R&D subsidiary of a diamond mining company. While our approach in this application starts with the theory developed in Chapter 3, the size of the organization is such that individual projects are considered rather than aggregate programs (product lines). Thus, investments can be varied continuously, but not without limits (as in Chapter 3).

We first formulate a general dynamic version of the selection problem, where several projects have to be chosen, given their costs of development and probabilities of success under a budget constraint. We then show under what conditions this problem can be approximated by a single period IP optimization problem. Acknowledging limited data availability, we approximate projects by *linear* return functions and propose a very simple project ranking that is optimal if the projects are of similar size (no single project dwarfs the others). Most importantly, the prioritization index of "dollars return per dollar of investment" can be graphically presented and is intuitive and transparent for managers.

Chapter 5 addresses the fact that project decisions do not always happen orderly at the annual or quarterly portfolio review. Rather, projects often "arrive" (e.g., an idea or an opportunity) one-by-one and require quick go/no go decisions. Thus, management needs to apply *admission policies*. In this chapter, we develop a dynamic admission policy for projects with a general distribution of return estimates arriving according to a Poisson process (with exponential inter-arrival times), and being developed by a multitude of exponential servers. We show that there is a value hurdle for projects to be accepted, and this value hurdle becomes less stringent the more NPD capacity the organization has available at the time. We derive in closed form that NPD capacity has decreasing returns.

Chapter 6 turns to ongoing projects during execution. We examine the research question of *how a scarce resource should be allocated among ongoing projects that compete for access to the resource, or how projects should be awarded priority during execution.* Static priorities based on initial "strategic assessments" are not sufficient because project progress is stochastic – a project that looks advantageous today may suffer a setback tomorrow. Project prioritization must change dynamically over time, and conflicts among project managers over access to the resource are common in project organizations.

We start with the multi-armed bandit (MAB) framework (Gittins and Jones 1972) and show that the optimal policy introduced by Gittins and Jones and Whittle (1980) applies if projects are independent of one another, and if project delays reduce all payoffs exponentially (discounting). In order to maximize the portfolio value, a manager should assign his critical resource to the project with the highest projected reward in the future. This policy continues to hold if there is a fixed cost associated with switching among projects, and only the threshold, that determines when to switch, changes.

However, when projects differ in their delay penalties, the optimal policy changes: the scarce resource should be allocated to the project with the highest total *delay loss as if* it were delayed until one of the other projects is completed. The priority index "pretends" that each project is delayed all the way until the prioritized project is completed, although the dynamic policy re-evaluates the prioritization after each period.

Finally, Chapter 7 summarizes lessons from this research. Figure 7.1 overviews the portfolio problem as posed in this book. Portfolio management must be embedded in the context of strategy (which is "messy" and not fully structured) and includes the three sub-problems of idea

screening, portfolio selection and project prioritization. For each, this
book attempts to develop qualitative "rules of thumb" that can guide
managers.

Chapter 2

WHAT HAS BEEN DONE SO FAR? REVIEW OF PREVIOUS WORK ON THE PORTFOLIO PROBLEM

1.   Introduction

This chapter offers a literature review of the project portfolio selection problem. We summarize several streams of research, which we categorize along the dimensions of static versus dynamic time considerations, and strategic versus operational level of decision making (Figure 2.1). The Figure shows that little theoretical work has been done at the strategic and dynamic levels of decision making, which is where the contribution of this book lies. We discuss the main findings and limitations of previous work in Section 2 for the operational decision making level and Section 3 for the strategic decision making level. Section 4 gives an example of a qualitative strategic "derivation" of a portfolio from the business strategy. Finally, Section 5 draws some implications of previous work for this book.

	Static	**Dynamic**
Operational	• Resource Constrained Scheduling Problem (RCSP), *Brucker et al. 1999, Demeulemeester and Herroelen 2002, Neumann et al. 2002* • Mathematical Programming Formulation Models, *Fox, Baker and Bryant 1984, Loch et al. 2001* • Multi-criteria decision making tools, *Brenner 1994* • Analytical Hierarchy Process models, *Liberatore 1987*	• Multi-Armed Bandit (MAB) models, *Gittins and Jones 1972, Whittle 1980, Asawa and Teneketzis 1996* • Dynamic Scheduling Models, *Smith 1956, Harrison 1975, Wein 1992, Van Mieghem 2000* • Optimal admission models, *Stidham 1985, Kleywegt and Papastavrou 1998, Lewis et al. 1999* • Economic models, *Weitzmann 1979, Fox and Baker 1985, Vishwanath 1992* • *Adler et al. 1995*
Strategic	• *Roussel et al. 1991* • Break-Even Times (BET), *House and Price 1991* • *Wheelwright and Clark 1992* • *Ali et al. 1993* • Net Present Value (NPV) analysis, *Hess 1993, Sharpe and Kellin 1998* • *Cooper et al. 1998*	• *Chikte 1977* • *Prastacos 1981* • *Nobeoka and Cusumano 1997* • *Jones 1999*

Figure 2.1.   Overview of Portfolio Selection Literature

2.   Operational Decisions

At the operational level, the total budget must be allocated among multiple ongoing projects, both statically (one-time) and dynamically (repeatedly, that is, once per year or per semester, or whenever a new project idea emerges).

Extensive literature exists on the resource-constrained scheduling problem (RCSP). This work has focused mainly on algorithmic solution procedures (see the recent literature review by Brucker *et al.* 1999; Demeulemeester and Herroelen 2002, Neumann *et al.* 2002). Brucker *et al.* (1999) observe that this literature has not sufficiently addressed task uncertainty. While recent work has focused on task uncertainty (Stork 2000; Demeulemeester and Herroelen 2002), it has again focused on algorithmic solutions and policy comparisons (due to problem complexity). However, as Stork 2000 puts it, "this literature is more scheduling and less dynamic programming". The current book, in contrast, emphasizes rules that are suggested by qualitative models, while characterizing the limits of how far analytical solutions can help us.

Along similar lines, there have been many attempts to model the resource allocation problem with mathematical programming formulations. One example is the extensive literature on knapsack formulations. This methodology has been examined in depth in Operations Research (OR) and is characterized by its many variants, applied in different companies (Beged-Dov 1965; Benson *et al.* 1993; Czajkowski and Jones 1986; Fox *et al.* 1984; Schmidt and Freeland 1992; Souder 1973; Souder 1978; Loch *et al.* 2001, Dickinson *et al.* 2001). In a recent contribution, Belhe and Kusiak 1997 build a multi-dimensional knapsack model of resource allocation across multiple project activities, considering a myopic decision maker who optimizes next period's allocation.

Although mathematical programming is a sound methodology for optimization problems, and it has been successfully applied in several specific cases, it has not found widespread acceptance by practitioners (Cabral-Cardoso and Payne 1996; Corbett and Van Wassenhove 1993; Gupta and Mandakovic 1992; Loch *et al.* 2001, Meredith 2001).

This gap stems partly from the complexity and sophistication of the methods, which are difficult to understand and to adopt for people who are not trained in OR, and partly from the lack of transparency and from the sensitivity of the results to changes of the problem parameters (for example, demonstrated for a mixed-integer programming application in Loch *et al.* 2001). In addition, mathematical programming formulations do not account for dynamic effects, such as the option to abandon some of the projects during development, or the fact that different projects start and end at different points in time. Chapter 4 addresses some of these limitations by proposing a methodology that couples OR theory (from Chapter 3) with a simple intuitive tool in an application of structuring the selection process in a diamond mining company.

Recently, Beaujon *et al.* 2001 made the observation, similar to the one in Chapter 3, that project funding is not a "zero or one" decision, but that it can be continuously adjusted. They propose linear programming as an approximation, consistent with our approach in Chapter 4.

In decision theory, many models rank projects via a composite average score on multiple "qualitatively" assessed dimensions, choosing the n best candidates for the portfolio (Brenner 1994; Loch 2000). Similarly, the analytical hierarchy process (AHP, see Liberatore 1987; Saaty 1994; Hammonds *et al.* 1998, Henriksen and Traynor 1999) is a structured process of multi-criteria decision making. However, multi-dimensional decision making methods lack a significant determinant of project choice, namely interactions among projects, both on the technical and on the market side.

Several authors have explored the dynamic portfolio selection decision emphasizing optimal policies rather than algorithmic solutions. Reflecting the uncertainty in projects, this work mostly considers stochastic settings. This literature comprises four groups.

The largest group is the multi-armed bandit (MAB) problem literature, which has strongly influenced the scheduling literature in Operations Research (OR). It was first solved by Gittins and Jones (1972), and since then, many variants have been proposed and solved by other researchers. The general formulation is described as follows: Consider K projects proceeding in parallel. A critical resource can be devoted to only one project at a time. This critical resource must be used by every project throughout. Time proceeds in discrete steps, $t = 0, 1, 2, 3, \ldots$. Project k's state at time t is $j_k(t)$. Working on project k returns an immediate reward $R_k(j_k(t))$. A project that is worked on undergoes Markovian transitions with known probabilities p_{ij}. The states of the projects that are not being worked on remain unchanged. Rewards are discounted with a factor $\beta \in (0, 1)$ per time unit. Gittins and Jones formulated the well-known *Gittins index*, a number that can be assigned to each project at each time t, and that characterizes the optimal policy. At any time t, it is optimal to work on the project with the highest Gittins index. In general, the Gittins index is difficult to compute, but the fact that the multi-armed bandit problem is *decomposable* simplifies the index. It depends only on each individual project's state (Bertsimas and Niño-Mora 1996) and corresponds to the reward that would make the decision maker indifferent as to whether to continue the project or exchange it for that reward.

The basic multi-armed bandit problem is described by Whittle (1980), Ross (1982) and Bertsimas and Niño-Mora (1996). Whittle (1980) and Ross (1982) proved that it is always optimal to work on the project with the highest index, defined as the salvage value that makes project continuation equally attractive to retirement.

The MAB policy rests upon a number of assumptions, which make policy extensions hard to obtain for more generic circumstances. Gittins (1989) showed that, for differing discount functions, there is no general index unless the functions are exponential (pp. 27-29. See also Nash 1980). Banks and Sundaram 1994, prove that the introduction of switching costs disrupts decomposability, hence no general index can be found.

Several of the assumptions on which the above results rest do not fit the characteristics of NPD projects, since costs occur over the entire project duration, while a reward is earned only after the project's outcome is launched onto the market. Moreover, delayed projects often suffer penalties in the market, which violates the assumption that a project's value function remains unchanged while it is not worked on.

In Chapter 6, we expand existing results to incorporate these characteristics of NPD, and provide limitations for policy extensions.

The second group of qualitative models approaches the prioritization problem as a multiclass queueing system, where different classes of jobs share a common server. Each job class requires a stochastic time on the server and incurs a linear delay cost. The main result is the "$c\mu$ rule" (Smith 1956; Cox and Smith 1961; Harrison 1975): give priority to the job with the highest delay cost divided by the expected processing time (marginal cost c, over time $\tau = \frac{1}{\mu}$). The rule is proven optimal for linear delay cost structures in various applications (Wein 1992; Ha 1997; Van Mieghem 2000).[1] For non-linear delay costs, the "generalized $c\mu$ rule" (G-$c\mu$) has been shown to be asymptotically optimal in heavy traffic (Van Mieghem 1995) and in due-date scheduling (also referred to as the "Generalized Largest Delay" rule in Van Mieghem 2001). Banerjee and Hopp 2001 have extended the $c\mu$ rule to job failures during processing, in a context without project performance states and with a single common discount rate (no differential levels of urgency).

The $c\mu$ rule can be viewed as a "continuous time" approximation of the Gittins index. Van Oyen *et al.* 1992 and Veatch and Wein 1996 have pointed out the similarity between bandit policies and the $c\mu$ rule.

The third group of work outlines optimal admission rules when a budget has to be allocated over time to project ideas. Chapter 5 is strongly

---

[1] Ha uses the name "$b\mu$ rule" in his context, where the equivalent of the delay cost is the backlog cost b.

related to this work. More specifically, Chapter 5 is related to the admission control problem in manufacturing systems (for an overview, see Stidham 1985; Miller 1969; Lippman and Ross 1971). Chapter 5 differs from manufacturing settings in two aspects: (i) The project attractiveness measure is continuous (there are uncountably many customer classes). (ii) Our system has a waiting buffer of size 1, from which the waiting project disappears when a new project idea arrives. In other words, the new idea is not turned away, but the old idea is superseded. This assumption represents project obsolescence, which is more important in NPD than in manufacturing. These model features lead to results that are consistent with recent literature (more available capacity lowers the threshold for acceptance, see, e.g., Stidham 1985, Lewis *et al.* 1999). We derive the decreasing thresholds and the optimal value function in closed form.

Chapter 5 is also related to previous research on reneging customers (the interpretation is usually that customers become impatient and leave after a while in the queue, but this phenomenon can also be interpreted as obsolescence). Usually, customers are assumed to renege with a certain probability either based on the amount of time they have spent waiting, or on the number of people in front of them in the queue. In particular, the time a customer waits in the queue is usually assumed as an exponential random variable (e.g., see the overview in Aksin and Harker 2001). However, in a portfolio setting, obsolescence arises from new ideas arriving (it is as if the waiting time in the queue was forced to have the same sample path as the arrival distribution).

Finally, the stochastic dynamic knapsack model, in which a given number of resource units is allocated to several classes of objects. These arrive according to a Poisson process until resources are exhausted. Kleywegt and Papastavrou 1998 show that if all items are of the same size, a threshold policy is optimal, the value function is concave in the remaining amount of resource, and the threshold increases as the resource is depleted. Kleywegt and Papastavrou 2001 show that the results generalize to the case of stochastic resource requirements of the items, but only if the resource requirement distribution fulfills certain conditions (concavity), and the terminal value function is concave nondecreasing.

The third and second groups of work share methodological foundations, but differ in the main research question: prioritization versus admission. An economics perspective on project choice is offered by Vishwanath 1992; Weitzman 1979 and Roberts and Weitzman 1981. Their work is the most closely related to our study in Chapter 3, and they derive optimal decision policies considering expected rewards and completion times of the projects, as well as their distribution functions. They do not consider intermediate project reviews (recourse) or delay penalties.

Fox and Baker 1985 examine the portfolio selection problem in a dynamic context. The complexity of their model forces them to use simulations in order to analyze the model's behavior. Similarly, Childs and Triantis 1999 describe different scenarios of project portfolios analyzed by simulation techniques, without discussing optimality.

Adler *et al.* 1995 adopt a different perspective and investigate a multi-project NPD organization as a queueing network, conceptualizing resources as "servers" processing the activities of various projects. They propose general congestion-reducing steps, such as static priorities and keeping the work-in-progress of projects constant, but consider neither dynamic project prioritization during execution, nor admission issues.

Finally, Goldratt 1997 argues heuristically that tasks competing for a common resource should *not* be interrupted once started, because doing so increases the total waiting suffered by the entire project portfolio. As a side result of our study in Chapter 6, we show under which circumstances Goldratt's rule of thumb is valid.

3.   Strategic Decisions

The NPD portfolio selection problem has attracted strategy and management research interest, reflecting its importance for top management decisions. Roussel *et al.* 1991 popularized the importance of portfolio selection for top management in organizations. Cooper *et al.* 1998 and Liberatore and Titus 1983 carried out a large survey of top management decision making concerning their NPD portfolios. Also, Wheelwright and Clark 1992a recognized the importance of portfolio selection for strategic decision making. They proposed two determinants, the product change level and the process change level introduced by an NPD project (see Figure 1.2). These tools have been heavily used in practice, as they facilitate useful discussions in managerial meetings (Loch 1996). A limitation of this work is that it is descriptive or based on a few examples; it does not provide a tool for understanding the implications of multi-period effects, of budget, and market interactions, since their analysis is predominantly static. An additional drawback of these methods is that they stay at a very aggregate level, without really assessing the exact balance that the R&D manager should keep in the portfolio.

On the theoretical side, Ali *et al.* 1993 model an R&D race between two firms that can choose to develop two different products. They model a simple competitive setting, and show the effect that competition has on project choice. Their one-shot approach does not account for the dynamic aspect of a firm's project portfolio and the carry-over impact of decisions into future developments.

A more practice-oriented approach encompasses findings from the financial literature like net present value (NPV) analysis (Hess 1993; Sharpe and Kellin 1998) and break-even time (BET) (House and Price 1991) applied at the operational level of a single project. Each project is assigned an index (its financial value), and these indices are ranked to determine the n best candidates.

There have not been many studies in a dynamic setting, where the presence of uncertainty and interactions lead to changes in the optimal allocation over time. Chikte 1977, models parallel development activities and corresponding resource allocation strategies. He assumes that investment in an activity impacts its probability of success, while we explicitly consider a return on investment function (Chapter 3). Moreover, Chikte analyzes general structural properties with no attempt to derive managerial decision rules. Prastacos 1981 considers investments over multiple periods with different returns (i.e., increasing or decreasing), but focuses on a single investment per period. He does not analyze the case of multiple projects competing for resources.

Nobeoka and Cusumano 1997 and Jones 1999 highlight the importance of multiple product line management for firm performance, but do not develop a normative theory. They offer empirical evidence from the automotive and the telecommunications industries.

There is also extensive literature on the dynamic financial portfolio problem (e.g., Merton 1969; Constantinides and Malliaris 1995; Samuelson 1969). Samuelson 1969 is closest to our treatment of the problem. He develops a multi-period investment model, albeit without obsolescence and interactions among projects. We do not address these financial models in detail here because they generally assume linear returns (e.g., number of stocks multiplied by stochastic prices), while the return on an NPD investment is non-linear in the amount of resources (e.g., Arthur 1994; Brooks 1975). Our model in Chapter 3 allows for non-linear returns without decomposition.

4. Strategic Alignment of R&D: an Example

A fundamental function of portfolios is to focus attention and to communicate the ambition and priorities of the organization. This is what Hamel and Prahalad 1989 called "strategic intent": envisioning a desired leadership position and establishing the criteria to chart progress. To achieve this, non-financial measures, which depend on the "type of success desired" (e.g., Hart 1993), are necessary.

The communicated goals determine which kinds of actions to take. A well-known tool for developing strategy-related performance measures is Kaplan and Norton's (1996) balanced scorecard, which explicitly recognizes that in addition to financial measures, operational measures (customer-related, process-related and learning-related) should be derived from the company's strategy. In a project at the diamond company GemStone,[2] we cascaded the business strategy down to R&D initiatives.

Based on the workshops with upper management, we could concisely summarize GemStone's business strategy by answering five questions, following Markides 1999: *what do we sell, to whom, how (with what core competence and processes), why (what is the value proposition to the customers and its competitive advantage), and what are the major threats in the environment?* The technology strategy, mirroring the business strategy, can be described along the same dimensions. It must specify

---

[2]The material in this section is based on Loch and Tapper 2002. The company, GemStone, is described in more detail in Section 2 of Chapter 4 in this book.

what technologies to master, and how these technologies relate to the business: what products and segments they address, and what they contribute to competitive advantage and to hedging against environmental threats. The technology strategy also has a "how": with what timing, and what risk profile are the products/processes delivered, and how does this program fit into the available set of resources? Figure 2.2 cascades GemStone's business strategy down to development and research strategies.

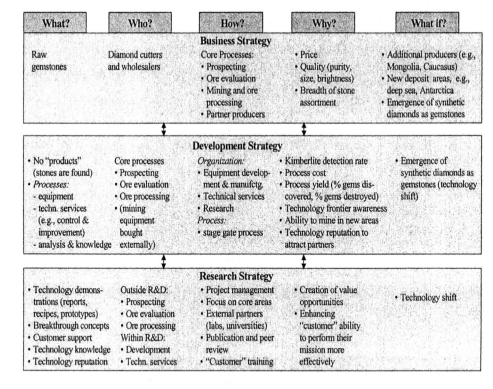

What?	Who?	How?	Why?	What if?
Business Strategy				
Raw gemstones	Diamond cutters and wholesalers	Core Processes: • Prospecting • Ore evaluation • Mining and ore processing • Partner producers	• Price • Quality (purity, size, brightness) • Breadth of stone assortment	• Additional producers (e.g., Mongolia, Caucasus) • New deposit areas, e.g., deep sea, Antarctica • Emergence of synthetic diamonds as gemstones
Development Strategy				
• No "products" (stones are found) • *Processes:* - equipment - techn. services (e.g., control & improvement) - analysis & knowledge	Core processes • Prospecting • Ore evaluation • Ore processing • (mining equipment bought externally)	*Organization:* • Equipment development & manufctg. • Technical services • Research *Process:* • stage gate process	• Kimberlite detection rate • Process cost • Process yield (% gems discovered, % gems destroyed) • Technology frontier awareness • Ability to mine in new areas • Technology reputation to attract partners	• Emergence of synthetic diamonds as gemstones (technology shift)
Research Strategy				
• Technology demonstrations (reports, recipes, prototypes) • Breakthrough concepts • Customer support • Technology knowledge • Technology reputation	Outside R&D: • Prospecting • Ore evaluation • Ore processing Within R&D: • Development • Techn. services	• Project management • Focus on core areas • External partners (labs, universities) • Publication and peer review • "Customer" training	• Creation of value opportunities • Enhancing "customer" ability to perform their mission more effectively	• Technology shift

Figure 2.2. GemStone's Business, Development and Research Strategy

GemStone produces essentially a commodity product, sold to diamond cutters based on quality, price, and the completeness of diamond varieties one has to offer. There are several potential threats to the industry structure (artificial diamonds, the emergence of new producers, and new deposit areas contemplated, if not yet utilized). GemStone is attempting to build an alliance of producers to strengthen their market position.

As GemStone does not produce diamonds, but finds and extracts them, innovation concerns only new processes, not new products. Thus, key contributions from new process development concern costs and yields in the core processes of prospecting, ore evaluation, and ore processing. R&D is also responsible for serving as a knowledge repository of new technologies and how they may affect the business, specifically to prepare the operating units for new areas of mining expected to emerge soon: under the sea and arctic mining . In addition, top management has formulated the mission to develop a technology leader reputation in order to become a more attractive potential partner to other producers.

This description of the *de facto* technology strategy was discussed with the research program managers. Building on this, they were able to formulate three types of outputs contributing to technology strategy:

- Technology demonstrations, that is, proof of feasibility and potential with working (hardware) prototypes, process recipes, or with technical reports proving a principle. This included, in particular, breakthrough concepts, or significant innovations with a large potential (e.g., identifying diamonds in the rock with X-ray radiation).

- Customer service, or training of personnel for technical services and plant engineering. This also includes serving as a second-line help desk for requests from the mines that the technicians in technical services cannot solve.

- Being a knowledge repository for the whole company about all technical aspects of diamond production, advising on high level decisions impacted by technology and on current trends. This includes building an external technology reputation via patents, conferences, publications, etc.

The research group decided to focus on core areas of expertise, to emphasize collaboration with external partners (universities and private labs), to strengthen project management, and to start evaluating external publications. Finally, they proposed to improve the cooperation with their "customers" by offering technical training, particularly for technical services.

The above analysis (strategy cascading) allowed the research group to (a) formulate a set of performance measures for the existing portfolio, which reflected the specific characteristics both of the strategic mission and of the work to be performed, and was adjusted to the risks so they could be seen by the employees as constructive and fair rather than as an instrument of control. (b) The group could formulate a collection of programs (a portfolio) that would improve the strategic rationale for the company (top-down), but would, at the same time, allow the researchers to formulate their own ideas and what these would contribute, even if not foreseen in current strategy (bottom-up).

The research group came to understand that R&D performance measures must reflect the activity portfolio. A strategic portfolio allows formulating a set of activities that embodies business strategy, while performance measures allow monitoring the progress and the value produced.

The thus derived portfolio not only aligns R&D efforts top-down, but it also allows bottom-up idea proposals within a structure. It educates researchers about the business needs of the organization and helps them to think strategically. Although the system must initially be derived top-down, it ultimately gives researchers a way to think about and categorize new ideas: recognize them as fitting the strategy, or express in what sense they do not fit the current strategy, but have a potential that could complement or modify it. As a result, the quality of communication between top management and researchers can be enhanced.

5.   Implications for this Book

Management researchers and practitioners have proposed many methodologies for tackling the complexity of the portfolio selection problem. The literature review suggests that quantitative research efforts have not been widely adopted in practice because of their complexity, and have partly ignored the dynamic nature and the interaction effects in portfolio selection decisions.

This book attempts to make a step toward including these effects; our critical assumption is that project decisions are not "zero-one" (go/no go), but continuous variables, that is, project budgets can be adjusted up or down. This allows us to connect project decisions to marginal returns, which, in turn, permits developing easier-to-use methods while including additional multi-period and interaction effects.

Chapter 3

DYNAMIC SELECTION OF NPD PROGRAMS

1. Introduction

Selecting program portfolios is an important challenge in the management of new product development (NPD). At the aggregate level of
business management, a key decision is the allocation of resources across
product lines or market segments.[1]

The complexity of the problem is partially driven by the assumption
(common to all methods used, and a common mindset among R&D
managers) that a project is "in" or "out". However, at the level of
a strategic business unit, top management typically does not discuss
every single technical project, but allocates funds to different product
lines. Thus, the allocation to a product line can be increased or reduced
(almost) continuously, increasing or reducing the expected profitability
accordingly. Even at the level of individual projects, such adjustment

---

[1]This chapter is based on Loch C. H., and S. Kavadias, 2002: "Dynamic Portfolio Selection
of NPD Programs Using Marginal Returns." *Management Science* 48 (10), 1227 - 1241.

can sometimes be done (e.g., Beaujon *et al.* 2001). Based on this insight, this article develops a dynamic programming model of portfolio choice in which *marginal analysis* is used to illuminate the qualitative structure of optimal policies. Our results make two contributions: on the theoretical side, we offer one of the first comprehensive models of strategic NPD resource allocation with closed-form solutions. On the managerial side, the solution characteristics can be translated into qualitative managerial guidelines. The model shows that the interactions of the influence parameters are subtle, partly non-intuitive, and complex. In a context where many important problem parameters can only be roughly estimated, qualitative rules based on a rigorous model may be the most effective way to help managers check their rules of thumb, and understand the directional impact of changes in technology or markets.

This chapter develops a dynamic model of resource allocation, taking into account multiple interacting factors, such as uncertain market payoffs that change over time, increasing or decreasing returns from the NPD investment, carry-over of the investment benefit over multiple periods, and interactions across segments.

We characterize the optimal policies in closed form and derive qualitative decision rules for managers. In the presence of increasing returns, the whole budget is optimally allocated to one product line, while decreasing returns lead to a split of the budget. The optimal allocation properties are subtle and partly counter-intuitive. For example, neither the longevity of the product line, nor market size in future periods always increase the investment. For a risk-averse decision maker, a higher variance in next period's market potential makes a product line less attractive, but a higher variance in a future period may increase the optimal allocation. If the product lines interact, the complement/substitution effect acts as an additional/reduced carry-over benefit.

We present the model set-up (Section 2), derive the basic results for increasing (Section 3) and decreasing returns (Section 4), and then analyze the extensions of risk aversion, market interactions and stochastic carry-over benefits (Sections 5-7). Section 8 provides an illustrative numerical example, and Section 9 shows how the 2-product and 2-period results extend to n products and T periods.

2.   Model Setup

Consider a firm that operates n different product lines. For example, an automobile firm develops three lines: compact cars, high-end sedans and light trucks. The total R&D, budget (typically 4-5% of sales in the car industry and up to 10% in telecommunications) must be allocated to these *programs* (product lines). Each product line sells in a separate (but not necessarily independent) market segment. The R&D division of the firm reviews its resource allocation after constant time intervals (e.g., every six months), $t = 0, 1, 2, ..., T$. In each period a new allocation decision takes place at the product line level. The Tth period is the end of the horizon, incorporating all possible information that top

management has about the distant future.[2]

The conditions of the n market segments are uncertain in each pe-

riod: the firm may face fewer or more competitors, or shifting customer

preferences. We model the conditions in market i $(1 \leq i \leq n)$ at time t

through *potential* market profits, representing the upper limit on profits

that the firm may possibly earn from a given market segment during a

given period (if the product is perfect under given competitive condi-

tions). This market potential is represented by a random variable with

expectation $E[\Pi_{it}]$.

The fraction of the potential profit that a product line can achieve

is represented by a return function $f_{i(t+1)}\left(\mu_i C_{i(t-1)} + c_{it}\right)$, where $C_{it} =$

$\mu_i C_{i(t-1)} + c_{it} = \sum_{n=0}^{t} \mu_i^n c_{i(t-n)}$ is the *effective investment* in the prod-

uct line. The effective investment consists not only of the resources

allocated in that period, c_{it}, but also of a carry-over $\mu_i C_{i(t-1)}$ from the

previous period's effective investment, which supports present period re-

turns. This reflects the fact that the benefit from an NPD investment

does not disappear from one period to the next, as the resulting products

live for a while. However, the investment does decay as time passes –

technology becomes obsolete, and brand reputation fades. The portion

$\mu_i \in [0, 1]$ of the carried-over investment may also reflect that some of

---

[2]Instead, one could choose a model with an infinite horizon and stationarity. In our experience, managers tend to think rather in terms of a finite horizon and non-stationarity, with
the last period representing the "long run".

the projects may take more than one review period to complete (in which case $\Pi_{it} = 0$ before market introduction, but $\mu_i = 1$ as product quality is built). The investment carry-over (and the obsolescence it may imply) are independent of the usual financial discounting over time. The latter is represented by a discount factor β per period.[3]

The functions $f_{it}(.)$ are period-specific and may have either increasing returns (convex functions) or decreasing returns (concave functions). They are product line properties, capturing a combination of market structures and technology characteristics.

The firm's objective is to allocate a set of predetermined NPD budgets $\{B_0, B_1, ..., B_{T-1}\}$ among the product lines, in order to maximize the value of its product line portfolio. For the purpose of exposition and readability, we assume from this point on that $T = 2$, and that there are 2 product lines. In Section 8 of this chapter, we show that our key result (Theorem 3.2) holds for multiple products and time periods and for a period-dependent carry-over μ_{it}.

The optimal investment is determined as the solution of a finite-horizon problem with 2 periods:

$$\max_{\substack{c_{10}+c_{20} \leq B_0 \\ c_{11}+c_{21} \leq B_1}} \{-\sum_i c_{i0} + \beta \sum_i [f_{i1}(c_{i0})E[\Pi_{i1}] - c_{i1}]$$

$$+\beta^2 \sum_i f_{i2}(\mu_i c_{i0} + c_{i1})E[\Pi_{i2}]\} \quad (3.1)$$

---

[3]The financial discount factor should reflect the *systematic* risk of the company (or major business unit), as captured by the weighted average cost of capital (WACC). Risk adjusted discounting is usually not applicable for R&D programs, as they are typically idiosyncratic and cannot be replicated by traded assets (e.g., Huchzermeier and Loch 2001; Dixit and Pindyck 1994, 121).

3.   Increasing Returns

This section analyzes the optimal investment policies for product lines with increasing returns. These characterize product lines that are in the accelerating part of the diffusion curve or are gaining market share because of economies of scale or high positive network externalities (e.g., Microsoft Excel replaced Lotus 1-2-3 after a long ramp-up phase within one year: an investment in market share may "build on itself", see e.g., Loch and Tapper 2002). Mathematically, increasing returns correspond to $f'_{it}(.) \geq 0$, and $f''_{it}(.) \geq 0$. With increasing returns, the optimization problem (3.1) has the following solution.

THEOREM 3.1 *It is optimal in every period to allocate the total budget to one product line.*

Proof All proofs are shown in the appendix.

The resulting policy transforms the initial optimization problem into one with a restricted choice set (in each period, either project may receive the whole budget). This problem is a restless bandit problem, since the states in each period change not only for the product line that is funded but also for the others (because of the effective investment decay). The restless bandit problem has not been solved in general (it is NP-hard) but there exist efficient algorithms for computing the optimal policies (see Bertsimas and Niño-Mora 2000).

In the special case without a carry-over benefit ($\mu_i = 0$ for all i), the maximization problem is a multi-armed bandit, since in each period one product line changes its status. Using the Gittins index (Gittins and Jones 1972; Whittle 1980), it is optimal to allocate the entire budget to the product line with the highest individual expected reward.

4.   Decreasing Returns

We now turn to the case where the investment return functions have decreasing returns. This is typically encountered in mature markets or with technologically mature product lines, situations that go with incremental innovation more than breakthroughs. Decreasing returns correspond to the conditions $f'_{it}(.) \geq 0$, and $f''_{it}(.) \leq 0$. We assume for now that the decision makers are risk neutral and the product lines do not influence one another (to be relaxed later). The optimal allocation is characterized in Theorem 3.2.

THEOREM 3.2 *It is optimal in every period to split the budget among the product lines according to their total marginal benefits (current and carried over into the future).*

$$\frac{f'_{12}(\mu_1 c_{10} + c_{11})}{f'_{22}(\mu_2(B_0 - c_{10}) + B_1 - c_{11})} = \frac{E[\Pi_{22}]}{E[\Pi_{12}]} \quad \text{(2nd period)} \qquad (3.2)$$

$$f'_{11}(c_{10})E[\Pi_{11}] - f'_{21}(B_0 - c_{10})E[\Pi_{21}]$$

$$+\beta(\mu_1 - \mu_2)f'_{12}(\mu_1 c_{10} + c_{11})E[\Pi_{12}] = 0 \quad \text{(1st period)}. \qquad (3.3)$$

If no solution to (3.2) and (3.3) exists, that is, if the total marginal benefits of the two products do not cross anywhere, then in each period, the budget is allocated to the product line with the higher total marginal benefit in that period.

$f'_{it}(\cdot)$ is the derivative of the return function with respect to its argument, the effective investment. The optimality conditions (3.2) and (3.3) represent the "total marginal benefit" in the respective period. It is optimal to invest in a product line up to the point where the total marginal benefit equals the marginal benefit obtained by investing in the "competing" product line. If in any period, one product line has a superior total marginal benefit over the entire budget range, it gets the whole budget.[4] Theorem 3.2 generalizes in a straightforward manner to multiple products and time periods with period-dependent μ_{it}: the budget is shared according to the total marginal benefits, including all future periods from the focal period on forward. Our result characterizes an optimal Dynamic Programming Policy: starting with the last period (the "distant future" summary period), calculate the marginal benefits and allocate the budget accordingly. Go back one period and calculate the total marginal benefits and the associated optimal allocation (using the future allocation calculated before), and so on. Each period, the decision makers can re-estimate the available data and recalculate the policy forward as new information becomes available.

---

[4]For simplicity, we assume independence of the potential market payoff Π_{it} over time. In the presence of dependence, the 2nd period equation (3.2) holds conditionally on the previous period's market realization.

The following Proposition describes the influence of each parameter in isolation through comparative statics, when the budgets are split. If one product receives all investment, then the investments are not impacted by marginal parameter changes.

PROPOSITION 3.1 *If the budgets are split, the optimal investment c_{it}^* has the properties:*

1. c_{it}^* increases in the marginal investment return $f_{it}'(\cdot)$, but not necessarily in the absolute investment return $f_{it}(\cdot)$.

2. It is myopically determined in both periods if the investment carry-over benefits are the same, $\mu_1 = \mu_2$.

3. It increases in the next period's potential payoff $\Pi_{i(t+1)}$. However, the first period's allocation c_{i0}^* decreases in Π_{i2} if product line i has a lower carry over benefit, $\mu_i < \mu_j$.

4. The first period's allocation c_{i0}^* increases in μ_i if $\mu_i < \mu_j$. If $\mu_i > \mu_j$, we can show that $c_{i0}|_{\mu_i > \mu_j} > c_{i0}|_{\mu_i = \mu_j}$.

5. Total allocation $c_{i0}^* + c_{i1}^*$ may not increase in the investment carry over μ_i.

6. If the budget is a decision variable, the optimal first period budget B_0^* increases in the carry over effects μ_i and μ_j, while the last period's budget B_1^* decreases. The total optimal budget may move in either direction. □

Claim 1 of Proposition 1 states that the classic logic of marginal investment applies here: one invests one more dollar into the product line until the *marginal* benefit is lower than for the other product line, even if the *absolute* benefit of the product line is higher for every amount of equal investment.

Claim 2 has an important relationship with results obtained in finance literature. Myopic allocation is known to be optimal in financial portfolios in the absence of carry-over benefits if investment returns are linear and utility has a log-form (Bertsekas 1997, 157). In our model, myopic decisions are still optimal under decreasing returns and with carry-over benefits, provided the latter are equal across the product lines.

Claim 3 of the proposition is counter-intuitive. The initial investment c_{i0}^* may *decrease* in the period-2 market potential Π_{i2} if it has a lower carry-over benefit. The explanation is that the decision maker should give more resources to the other product line j *now*, exploiting its higher carry-over, and react to the potential profit increase in product line i in the last period by *then* giving it more resources. Benefits down the line shift current investments toward projects with a longer-term horizon (higher carry-over).

Claim 4 is intuitive – if the carry-over benefit increases, the incentive for investing in the first period grows. However, this effect runs into diminishing returns – it may not be true that c_{i0}^* continues to monotonically increase in μ_i if $\mu_i > \mu_j$. Claim 5 can be explained by the effect of the third term in condition (3.3). The quantity $\mu_1 - \mu_2$ increases in

μ_1, while the rest of the term decreases in μ_1 because $f_{12}(\mu_1 c_{10} + c_{11})$ is concave. Thus, depending on the specific values of both the functions and the carry over effects, a higher carry-over benefit may optimally lead to "frontloading" and then "milking"of the product line.

We have taken the budget as a given parameter until now, reflecting the widespread practice of setting it as an industry-typical percentage of sales ("we cannot afford a higher R&D percentage of sales than our competitors" – statement by an executive). The 6th claim is relevant when the budget is a decision variable, and it is somewhat counter-intuitive. An increase in the carry-over benefit increases the optimal period one budget, but decreases the optimal future period investment (it leads to frontloading and then milking). This result implies that stable markets with little obsolescence may optimally have a *lower* total R&D investment than markets with fast obsolescence.

What happens when the carry-over μ_i is uncertain? This situation typically arises in new markets where customer loyalty is not known, where the speed of technology obsolescence may vary, or where project completion time may vary significantly.

Suppose an investment in product line 1 offers a high carry-over benefit $\mu'_1 = \mu_1^H$ with probability p, and a low carry-over $\mu'_1 = \mu_1^L$ with $1-p$. In order to make a fair comparison to the deterministic carry-over, we assume $E[\mu'_1] = \mu_1$. Theorem 3.2 tells us that the optimal allocation when μ_1 is deterministic. The optimality conditions become

$$\frac{f'_{12}(\mu_1^H c_{10} + c_{11}^H)}{f'_{22}(\mu_2(B_0 - c_{10}) + B_1 - c_{11}^H)} = \frac{E[\Pi_{22}]}{E[\Pi_{12}]} \text{ (with probability } p)$$

$$\frac{f'_{12}(\mu_1^L c_{10} + c_{11}^L)}{f'_{22}(\mu_2(B_0 - c_{10}) + B_1 - c_{11}^L)} = \frac{E[\Pi_{22}]}{E[\Pi_{12}]} \text{ (with probability } 1 - p)$$

for the last period, and

$$f'_{11}(c_{10})E[\Pi_{11}] - f'_{21}(B_0 - c_{10})E[\Pi_{21}] + \beta p_1(\mu_1^H - \mu_2)f'_{12}(\mu_1^H c_{10} + c_{11}^H)E[\Pi_{12}]$$

$$+ \beta(1 - p_1)(\mu_1^L - \mu_2)f'_{12}(\mu_1^L c_{10} + c_{11}^L)E[\Pi_{12}] = 0$$

for the first period. Proposition 3.2 compares the resulting optimal policy with the case of a deterministic carry-over.

PROPOSITION 3.2 *The optimal first-period allocation to a product line is smaller for an uncertain carry over benefit than when the carry-over is known.*

The intuition of Proposition 3.2 is a "wait and react" policy: invest less in period one, and possibly make up for the shortfall in period 2 if a large carry-over is revealed. This has the flavor of a "real option" – since it is possible to react in the second period, it is optimal to respond to the carry-over uncertainty by holding back in the first period.[5] To keep notation simple, we now go back to known carry-overs, generalizing the model to market dependence and risk aversion.

---

[5]This extends to a continuous distribution of μ if f_{it} is quadratic, implying generality for local disturbances of the carry-over (as the quadratic is the Taylor approximation of general functions). We have shown the global result for exponential, log and $x/(x + a)$ return functions, but not in general (nor are there, after extensive simulation, counterexamples).

5. Decreasing Returns and Market Interactions

In this section, we allow synergies across the two product lines, which might arise from common "enabling" projects or from important inter-dependencies in the market. For example, a car manufacturer may find that a popular high-end truck draws potential buyers of the entry-level car.

We model the interaction with a synergy parameter λ_i denoting the (delayed) influence of product line i investment on product line j. A positive λ_i corresponds to a complementary benefit, a negative λ_i to a substitution damage.[6] The effective investment of product line i includes this synergy: $C_{i1} = \mu_i c_{i0} + c_{i1} + \lambda_j c_{j0}$. The new total payoff function is as follows.

$$\max_{\substack{c_{10}+c_{20}\leq B_0 \\ c_{11}+c_{21}\leq B_1}} \{-\sum_i c_{i0} + \beta \sum_i f_{i1}(c_{i0})E[\Pi_{i1}] - \beta \sum_i c_{i1}$$
$$+\beta^2 \sum_{i\neq j} f_{i2}(\mu_i c_{i0} + \lambda_j c_{j0} + c_{i1})E[\Pi_{i2}]\}. \qquad (3.4)$$

As in Section 4, the solution can be found by maximizing the equivalent Langrangean, as we are operating at the budget constraints.

THEOREM 3.3 *When markets are interdependent, the optimal allocation is given by applying Theorem 2 to the following transformation for the second period return functions.*

$$\phi_{12}(x) = f_{12}(x + \lambda_2 B_0) \text{ and } \phi_{22}(x) = f_{22}(x + \lambda_1 B_0)$$

---

[6]If all product lines interact with one another dynamically over time, the interaction index becomes λ_{ijt}. In practice, there are often a few prominent interactions on which attention is focused – see the example in Section 8 and also Loch *et al.* 2001.

and carried over benefits $\mu'_1 = \mu_1 - \lambda_2$ and $\mu'_2 = \mu_2 - \lambda_1$.

The Theorem says that the cross product line synergy boosts the allocation similarly to an additional carry-over effect. Strictly speaking, the synergy λ_i does not directly increase that product line's carry-over, but decreases the "transformed" carry over of the competing product line. However, it is easy to show that claims 2, 4, and 5 of Proposition 3.1 generalize to this case, and can be expressed in terms of $\mu_i + \lambda_i$, a "composite" carry over effect. The synergy parameter affects the optimal allocation the same way as an additional carry-over benefit (or penalty). Thus, the effect of the synergy can be interpreted as an addition to the carry over benefit.

6.   Decreasing Returns and Risk Aversion

In this section we extend the model to incorporate managerial risk aversion. The carryover μ denotes now the transformed carryover with the new (shifted) functions, including market interaction effects: $\mu_i - \lambda_j$ in the notation of the last section.[7]

The decision maker has a utility function $u(x)$ with the level of net revenues as the argument. We make the standard assumptions from the financial literature (starting with Merton 1969) that $u(\cdot)$ is concave increasing: $u'(\cdot) > 0$ and $u''(\cdot) < 0$. With this utility function, the

---

[7]Since the transformation for market interaction shifts the origin of the return functions, the utility would have to be recalibrated to take into account the wealth effect. We omit the details.

portfolio allocation problem (3.1) becomes

$$\max_{\substack{c_{10}+c_{20}\leq B_0 \\ c_{11}+c_{21}\leq B_1}} E[u\{(-c_{10}-c_{20})+\beta\overline{\overline{\Pi}}_{t=1}+\beta(-c_{11}-c_{21})+\beta^2\overline{\overline{\Pi}}_{t=2}\}], \text{ where}$$

$$\overline{\overline{\Pi}}_{t=1}=\sum_i f_{i1}(c_{i0})\Pi_{i1} \text{ and } \overline{\overline{\Pi}}_{t=2}=\sum_i f_{i2}(\mu_i c_{i0}+c_{i1})\Pi_{i2},$$

$$\Pi_{total}=(-c_{10}-c_{20})+\beta\overline{\overline{\Pi}}_{t=1}+\beta(-c_{11}-c_{21})+\beta^2\overline{\overline{\Pi}}_{t=2},$$

and the expectation is defined over the probability distributions of the market potentials. The solution can be found by maximizing the equivalent Langrangean, as we are operating at the budget constraints (as in Section 4). This yields the following Theorem.

THEOREM 3.4 *It is optimal in every period to split the total budget among the product lines according to the conditions*

$$\frac{f'_{12}(\mu_1 c_{10}+c_{11})}{f'_{22}(\mu_2(B_0-c_{10})+B_1-c_{11})}=\frac{E[u'(\Pi_{total})\Pi_{22}]}{E[u'(\Pi_{total})\Pi_{12}]} \quad (3.5)$$

$$f'_{11}(c_{10})E[u'(\Pi_{total})\Pi_{11}]-f'_{21}(B_0-c_{10})E[u'(\Pi_{total})\Pi_{21}] \quad (3.6)$$
$$+\beta(\mu_1-\mu_2)f'_{12}(\mu_1 c_{10}+c_{11})E[u'(\Pi_{total})\Pi_{12}]=0$$

Thus, Theorem 3.2 can be re-expressed in terms of equal utility benefits.

Conditions (3.5) and (3.6) describe the optimal allocation without any distributional assumptions. In the following Proposition, we analyze the comparative statics of the optimal solution. In order to explicitly incorporate variance as a representation of uncertainty, we make two additional assumptions: (i) market potentials are uncorrelated normal distributions (relaxed later) and (ii) the utility function is the standard negative exponential with constant risk aversion (Merton 1969): $u(x) = \frac{1}{a} - \frac{1}{a}\exp(-ax)$. Using the well-known identity: If $X \sim N(\mu, \sigma^2)$ then $Y = e^X \sim LN(\mu, \sigma^2)$, we can write the utility function as

$$
\begin{aligned}
E[u(x)] \quad &= E[\tfrac{1}{a} - \tfrac{1}{a}\exp(-ax)] \\
&= \tfrac{1}{a} - \tfrac{1}{a}\exp(-aE[x] + \tfrac{1}{2}a^2 Var[x]), \text{ and by independence:} \\
E[u(\Pi_{total})] \quad &= \tfrac{1}{a} - \tfrac{1}{a}\exp(-B_0 - \beta B_1) \\
&\prod_{i,t}\left(\exp(-a\beta^t f_{it}(.)E[\Pi_{it}] + \tfrac{1}{2}a^2\beta^{2t}f_{it}^2(.)Var[\Pi_{it}])\right).
\end{aligned}
$$

This allows us to transform the general conditions (3.5) and (3.6) to

$$
\frac{f_{12}'(\mu_1 c_{10} + c_{11})}{f_{22}'(\mu_2(B_0 - c_{10}) + B_1 - c_{11})}
$$
$$
= \frac{E[\Pi_{22}] - a\beta^2 f_{22}(\mu_2(B_0 - c_{10}) + B_1 - c_{11})Var[\Pi_{22}]}{E[\Pi_{12}] - a\beta^2 f_{12}(\mu_1 c_{10} + c_{11})Var[\Pi_{12}]}; \qquad (3.7)
$$

$$
\begin{aligned}
&f_{11}'(c_{10})\{E[\Pi_{11}] - a\beta^2 f_{11}(c_{10})Var[\Pi_{11}]\} \\
-\ &f_{21}'(B_0 - c_{10})\{E[\Pi_{21}] - a\beta^2 f_{21}(B_0 - c_{10})Var[\Pi_{21}]\} \\
+\ &\beta(\mu_1 - \mu_2)f_{12}'(\mu_1 c_{10} + c_{11})\{E[\Pi_{12}] - a\beta^2 f_{12}(\mu_2 c_{10} + c_{11})Var[\Pi_{12}]\} \\
=\ &0. \qquad\qquad\qquad\qquad\qquad\qquad\qquad\qquad\qquad\qquad\qquad\qquad (3.8)
\end{aligned}
$$

To assure that the utility function always has a positive argument, we assume $E[\Pi_{it}] - a\beta^t f_{it}(.)Var[\Pi_{it}] > 0$ (each project produces non-negative wealth).

PROPOSITION 3.3 *The optimal allocation c_{i0}^* has the following properties:*

1. It is larger when $\mu_i > \mu_j$, than when $\mu_i = \mu_j$.

2. It decreases in the variance of its first period market potential Π_{i1}.

3. It decreases (increases) in the variance of the second period market potential Π_{i2} if $\mu_i > \mu_j$ (if $\mu_i < \mu_j$).

The first result is a generalization of Proposition 3.1: a higher carry-over benefit increases the optimal early investment. The second result is also as expected: a risk averse manager should invest less into a product line with higher risk in the immediately following period (this holds both for initial investment under period-one risk and period one investment under period-two risk). The third result is surprising at first: higher riskiness of the period 2 market potential decreases period 0 investment for the product line with the higher carry-over benefit while boosting it for the product line with the lower carry over. An increase in variance prompts the decision maker to allocate initial investment to the other product line with less exposure to the second period – this is again the shifting of current resources due to longer-term risks and opportunities. A static risk-return matrix does not "see" this effect and may lead to incorrect conclusions.

In Proposition 3.4, we examine how correlation influences the optimal allocation. Suppose Π_{1t} and Π_{2t} are correlated with covariance $Cov[\Pi_{1t}, \Pi_{2t}]$. The expectation of the total utility is then (the dot in the formula indicates multiplication):

$$E[u(\Pi_{total})] = \frac{1}{a} - \frac{1}{a}\exp(-B_0 - \beta B_1)\bullet$$

$$\prod_t \left(\exp(-a\beta^t \sum_i f_{it}(.)E[\Pi_{it}] + \frac{1}{2}a^2\beta^{2t}\sum_i f_{it}^2(.)Var[\Pi_{it}]) + a^2\beta^{2t}f_{1t}(.)f_{2t}(.)Cov[\Pi_{1t},\Pi_{2t}])\right).$$

The covariance adds a term to the U_i's in the optimality conditions:

$$U_{it} = E[\Pi_{it}] - a\beta^2 f_{it}(.)Var[\Pi_{it}] - a\beta^2 f_{it}(.)f_{jt}(.)Cov[\Pi_{it},\Pi_{jt}].$$

To avoid degenerate cases, we assume a limit on the likelihood of a loss: $E[\Pi_{it}] - a\beta^2 Var[\Pi_{it}] - a\beta^2 Cov[\Pi_{it},\Pi_{jt}] > 0$. For tractability, let us also assume that more investment yields decreasing returns in utility everywhere, or $f_{it}''(.)U_{it} - a\beta^2 f_{it}'(.)Var[\Pi_{it}] + a\beta^2 f_{it}'(.)f_{jt}'(.) \, Cov[\Pi_{it},\Pi_{jt}] < 0$.

PROPOSITION 3.4 *Correlation among the product lines' payoff potentials influences the optimal allocation c_{i0}^* as follows. First, c_{i0}^* decreases in the covariance of the first period payoffs, if the derivative of $f_{i1}(.)f_{j1}(.)$ is positive in the optimal solution. Second, c_{i0}^* decreases in the covariance of the second period payoffs if $\mu_i > \mu_j$.*

The intuition of claim 1 is explained as follows: The covariance term represents an additional source of risk for the risk-averse decision maker. Hence, the reaction to it is negative for the product line that contributes more of that risk if we increase its resources (recall that the extent to which covariance contributes to overall risk is $a\beta^2 f_{it}(.)f_{jt}(.)Cov[\Pi_{it},\Pi_{jt}]$). The quantity $f_{i1}'(.)f_{j1}(.) - f_{i1}(.)f_{j1}'(.)$ identifies exactly this: the difference between the product lines' contribution to the overall risk.

The explanation of the second claim is similar to the effect of the second period variance in Proposition 3.3. Potential payoff covariance reduces the possibility of hedging across product lines and thus has the same effect as an additional source of variance, which the risk-averse decision maker wants to avoid.

7. Numerical Example

We now illustrate our model with a numerical example of four products, based on a real situation from the diamond industry. The data have been simplified and disguised for confidentiality purposes (for details, see Kavadias *et al.* 2003). The company's portfolio involves four major research programs: A and X concern the efficiency of diamond retrieval from the ore; C and D are environmental programs that aim to reduce soil and water waste in diamond mines.

Return on investment has a natural concave form in each program. When asked, the managers were able to sketch a return function resulting from the most attractive projects being included first and the less attractive ones afterward, although returns were not conceptualized or reported this way. For exposition purposes, we approximate this by concave continuous return functions $f_{it}(x) = 1 - \exp(-\alpha_i x)$, as is summarized in Figure 3.1. The parameter α is set in such a way that 50-60% of the originally set budget of the program achieves 80% of the "nominal" benefit. The additional benefit of increasing the program budget beyond the originally agreed upon level yields a very small return. This is consistent with management's estimates (although it was not included in official reports).

	Return function (1)	Exp. payoff (1)	μ	λ	Return function (2)	Exp. payoff (2)
A	$1 - e^{(-0.01x)}$	50	0	0.5	$1 - e^{(-0.01x)}$	0
X	$1 - e^{(-0.02x)}$	200	0.2	0	$1 - e^{(-0.02x)}$	250
C	$1 - e^{(-0.03x)}$	100	0.5	0	$1 - e^{(-0.03x)}$	150
D	$1 - e^{(-0.04x)}$	250	0	0	$1 - e^{(-0.04x)}$	0

Figure 3.1.   Program Data for Numerical Example

Periods (1) and (2) in Figure 3.1 indicate *generations* of each program, each lasting three years (within a period, individual projects could be added or modified, but no new major programs were foreseen). Management specified three cross-period effects of resource allocations: the technological platform of A offered a substantial contribution to the development of the future generation of X (corresponding to λ_{AX} in our model). About 20% of the first generation investment in X affected its second generation benefit (μ_X). Finally, 50% of C's first generation investment would positively impact the benefit generated in the second generation (μ_C).

We first examine a scenario where management is risk neutral. Here, we simply use the payoff expectations (each program is normally distributed with mean payoff as the one in Figure 3.1 and variance $\sigma_i^2 = \sigma^2 = 900$). The results are summarized in Figure 3.2.

	A(1)	X(1)	C(1)	D(1)	X(2)	C(2)
λ=0.5	0.62	7.71	6.18	5.49	4.92	1.08
λ=2.0	5.07	6.16	3.59	5.18	0.34	5.66

Figure 3.2. Optimal Allocation in the Risk Neutral Scenario

The optimal investments in this example illustrate the theoretical insights of the model (Theorem 3.3): At the optimal solution, the marginal benefits across the four programs are equal (e.g., \$11.41 per additional dollar invested in the first generation, and \$12.89 in the second generation for the case $\lambda = 0.5$). The second line in Figure 3.2 shows what happens with a higher cross benefit λ_{AX}: A becomes more important as a portfolio value contributor, thus increasing its initial allocation, while X's second period allocation decreases. With a higher composite carryover $(\lambda + \mu)$, the total effective investment in X increases, and hence, resources are transferred to C.

Figure 3.3 illustrates the effect of risk aversion and correlations. Suppose the decision maker values returns according to the standard exponential

	A(1)	X(1)	C(1)	D(1)	X(2)	C(2)
λ=0.5	0.95	7.45	6.29	5.31	5.00	1.00
λ=2.0	1.03	7.39	6.32	5.26	4.80	1.20

Figure 3.3. Optimal Allocation in the Risk Averse Scenario

utility function from Finance Theory $u(W) = 1000(1 - \exp(-0.001W))$ (Merton 1969). Now it becomes important that X and D are correlated with $\rho = 50\%$. The correlation stems from the fact that they will be applied at the same mines around the same time and are, thus, equally affected by the same organizational risk factors. To keep the analysis simple, we take the first period program benefits as approximately deterministic (which is reasonable as they come earlier and can, thus, be better estimated).

The second line in Figure 3.3 shows that an increasing second-period correlation between the two programs implies a higher initial allocation to the product lines with the relatively higher (total) carryover effect, in this case, A, X, and C (Proposition 3.4), while the fourth program D (with no carry over benefit) receives a smaller allocation.

Managers are often used to saying "yes" or "no" to program funding proposals (following an integer programming mindset) and find this type of analysis surprising. The above example shows that our marginal benefit approach has a natural economic interpretation and allows to recognize systematic effects of cross-program and carry-over benefits. These qualitative results can be used as rules of thumb even when the optimization problem is too complex to be solved exactly.

8. n Product Lines and T Periods

The scope of this section is to establish that the initial assumption of only two product lines and two time periods is expositional and can be generalized. We return to a risk-neutral decision maker to keep notation manageable, and we take the budget constraint as fixed and binding.

THEOREM 3.5 *Suppose the allocation is over n product lines and T periods. The optimal allocation is determined by $(n-1)$ pairwise comparisons of marginal benefits with one "reference" product line (taken here as line n) at every period t. For every $i = 1, 2, ..., n-1$:*

$$\frac{f'_{iT}(\mu_{i(T-1)}C_{i(T-2)} + c_{i(T-1)})}{f'_{nT}(\mu_{n(T-1)}C_{n(T-2)} + B_T - \sum_{k=1}^{n-1} c_{k(T-1)})} = \frac{E[\Pi_{nT}]}{E[\Pi_{iT}]} \text{ (last period);} \qquad (3.9)$$

$$f'_{1t}(\mu_{i(t-1)}C_{i(t-2)} + c_{i(t-1)})E[\Pi_{it}] - f'_{nt}(\mu_{n(t-1)}C_{n(t-2)} + B_t \qquad (3.10)$$

$$- \sum_{k=1}^{n-1} c_{k(t-1)}E[\Pi_{nt}] + \beta(\mu_{it} - \mu_{nt})f'_{i(t+1)}(\mu_{it}C_{i(t-1)} + c_{it})E[\Pi_{1(t+1)}]$$

$$+ \sum_{k=t+2}^{T} \beta^{k-t}[\prod_{m=t+1}^{k} \mu_{im}](\mu_{ik} - \mu_{nk})f'_{ik}(\mu_{i(k-1)}C_{i(k-2)} + c_{i(k-1)})E[\Pi_{1k}] = 0,$$

the latter for the first $T-1$ periods $((t = 1, ..., T-1)$; μ_{it} carries over the investment benefit from period $t-1$ to period t in product line i) the definition of C_{it} is given in Section 3, and $C_{nt} = \mu_{nt}C_{n(t-1)} + B_t - \sum_{k=1}^{n-1} c_{kt}$). If a solution to (3.9) and (3.10) does not exist for all n product lines, then a subset of the product lines have equal marginal

benefits (i.e., receive a positive amount of resources) while the rest receive
$c_{it} = 0$. *In the extreme case where one product line has a higher marginal*
benefit than all others, it receives the full budget.

Theorem 3.5 generalizes Theorem 3.2 in a straightforward way. In the
presence of n product lines, one of the product lines functions as the
reference for all the others, and the optimal allocation equalizes the
marginal benefits of all product lines by setting them to the same as
the reference. Over T periods, the allocation in each period equates
the total marginal benefits, current plus carried over into the remaining
periods. Theorem 3.5 shows that the key result, the equal marginal
benefits condition, generalizes directly from the 2 product, 2 period case.
The considerations for sensitivity analysis also stay the same, but they
become much messier because multiple decision variables interact.

9.   Discussion and Conclusion

This chapter has developed a dynamic programming model of new product portfolio selection in NPD. The unit of analysis is not the single
project, but the strategic program associated with an entire product
line. Resource allocation at this level can most often be varied continuously because individual projects are small relative to the program.
This insight allows a *marginal benefit* analysis instead of combinatorial
optimization.

Our model extends existing theory by offering a closed form characterization of the optimal policy in the presence of a number of important dimensions, namely the product line return function, the potential size of the market segment, multiple period consequences (carry-over benefits) of the NPD investment, competition for a restricted common pool of resources, complementarity or substitution effects across product lines, and finally managerial risk aversion.

On the managerial side, our mathematical results imply robust decision "rules of thumb". Imagine a business unit allocating NPD resources among several product lines, each consisting of many candidate projects, including new products and some product support projects. The benefit of investment in one program is naturally concave, as the most attractive projects are included first, and the least attractive last.

If return functions are convex, one "winner takes all" (up to the resource level that a program can efficiently absorb). If returns are concave, invest in one program until the last project included is as attractive (has the same return) as the last project included in the other programs. Benefits that arise only in the long term should impact the allocation decision already this period (unless all product lines have the same carryover of a current dollar investment, in which case we can disregard the future and include this period's payoffs only). If investment in one program helps another program through synergies, that benefit should be included in the same manner as a future benefit for the program itself.

A negative change in long term prospects (such as market potential, or, if management is risk averse, market variance or correlation) should shift today's resources toward programs that are more focused on the short term (have less long-term exposure), and a positive long-term change has the opposite effect. Uncertainty in the long-term prospects of a program reduces its optimal allocation. These rules of thumb are intuitively appealing and had not yet been shown to hold at this level of generality.

Our insights are numerically illustrated on the applied research portfolio of a diamond producing company. A marginal analysis can be performed at the level of research programs. Our insights are sometimes applicable even at the level of individual projects, where marginal benefits can serve as a heuristic that helps build management intuition (see Kavadias *et al.* 2003).

Our model generalizes widely used qualitative tools, such as risk-return matrices or market segment balances. For example, the effect of risk depends on its return and the programs' time horizons. Static qualitative tools are unable to capture such multi-period effects. A lack of accurate data in NPD renders numerical model analyses non-reliable, as mis-estimates of multiple parameters may interact to an extent that cannot be captured by sensitivity analysis. Thus, well-understood qualitative solution characteristics such as the ones shown in our model are useful in practice.

Our model will extend to the co-existence of programs with convex and concave returns: we hypothesize that the best convex projects will be each given the upper limit of the resources they can absorb (Theorem 3.1), until the next convex program has a lower marginal benefit than the concave projects among which the remaining budget would be shared (Theorem 3.2). An elaboration of this procedure may be possible for projects with convex-concave return functions as fruitful future work. Further research should also examine optimal allocation when market potential payoffs are Markov chains, as well as include Bayesian updating of market potentials. The approach of marginal analysis may offer some important insights and robust rules of thumb for managers.

APPENDIX 3.A

Proof of Theorem 3.1. The Langrangean for the optimization problem (3.1) is:

$$L(c_{01}, c_{20}, c_{11}, c_{21}, \nu_0, \nu_1) = -\sum_i c_{i0} + \beta \sum_i f_{i1}(c_{i0})E[\Pi_{i1}] - \beta \sum_i c_{i1}$$

$$+\beta^2 \sum_i f_{i2}(\mu_i c_{i0} + c_{i1})E[\Pi_{i2}] + \nu_0(B_0 - c_{10} - c_{20}) + \nu_1(B_1 - c_{11} - c_{21}),$$

where ν_0, ν_1 are the Langrangean multipliers. The solution results from the first order Kuhn-Tucker conditions: $c_{it}\frac{\partial L}{\partial c_{it}} = 0$, and $\frac{\partial L}{\partial c_{it}} \geq 0$ for $i = 1, 2$ and $t = 0, 1$; as well as $\nu_j\frac{\partial L}{\partial \nu_j} = 0$, and $\frac{\partial L}{\partial \nu_j} \geq 0$ for $j = 1, 2$.

The solution vector of these equations is either an interior point if $c_{it} > 0$, or an extreme point (that is, some $c_{it} = 0$ and some do not). This is determined by the second order conditions, taking into account which constraints are active. Hence, for

$c_{20} = B_0 - c_{10}$ and $c_{21} = B_1 - c_{11}$, i.e., both constraints are active,

$$\frac{\partial^2 L}{\partial c_{10}^2} = \beta f_{11}''(c_{10})E[\Pi_{11}] + \beta f_{21}''(B_0 - c_{10})E[\Pi_{21}] + \beta^2 \mu_1^2 f_{12}''(\mu_1 c_{10} + c_{11})E[\Pi_{12}]$$

$$+ \beta^2 \mu_2^2 f_{22}''(\mu_2(B_0 - c_{10}) + B_1 - c_{11})E[\Pi_{22}]. \qquad (3.A.1)$$

Inspection shows that this expression is always positive. Thus, the interior point is a minimum rather than a maximum given that the return functions are convex, and the determinant of the Hessian is positive (we omit the detailed algebraic calculations. They can be obtained from the authors). Thus, the maximum is at the boundary for all periods, that is, $\sum_i c_{it} = B_t$. $\qquad \square$

Proof of Theorem 3.2. The proof follows the same steps as the proof of Theorem 1. In contrast to Theorem 1, equation (3.A.1) above and concavity of f_{it} implies $\partial^2 L / \partial c_{10}^2 \leq 0$, while the determinant of the Hessian is still positive. Thus, the interior point solution is now the portfolio maximizing allocation, given of course that for the given budgets there can be such an interior point. The first order conditions (3.2) and (3.3) give the solution. In the case where an interior solution to the system of Kuhn-Tucker conditions does not exist, it is obvious through the formulas that the total budgets are going to be allocated to one product line. In the last period, the dominant product line in terms of marginal benefit receives full budget. In the first period, total marginal benefits have to be compared. $\qquad \square$

Proof of Proposition 3.1. We prove all the properties stated below only for c_{1t}^*, due to the symmetry of the setup. To prove claim 1, suppose that $\mu_1 = \mu_2 = \mu$, $f_{11}(x) = f_{21}(x)$ for every x, and same payoff potentials in the first period (to ease exposition; this can be generalized with the same line of argument). According to (3.2) the optimal allocation satisfies:

$$f_{12}'(\mu c_{10} + c_{11})E[\Pi_{21}] - f_{22}'(\mu(B_0 - c_{10}) + B_1 - c_{11})E[\Pi_{22}] = 0.$$

Assume without loss of generality that $f_{12}(x) > f_{22}(x)$ for every $x \in [0, B_0 + B_1]$. This implies $c_{10}^* = \frac{B_0}{2}$. Then the last period condition becomes $f_{12}'(\mu \frac{B_0}{2} + c_{11})E[\Pi_{21}] -$

$f'_{22}(\mu\frac{B_0}{2} + B_1 - c_{11})E[\Pi_{22}] = 0$. But the general nature of the last period return functions on the investment implies that we may have the following three cases:

1) $f'_{12}(x) > \frac{E[\Pi_{22}]}{E[\Pi_{12}]} f'_{22}(x)$ for every $x \in [0, B_0 + B_1]$

2) $f'_{12}(x^*) = \frac{E[\Pi_{22}]}{E[\Pi_{12}]} f'_{22}(x^*)$ for some $x^* > \mu\frac{B_0}{2} + \frac{B_1}{2}$

3) $f'_{12}(x^*) = \frac{E[\Pi_{22}]}{E[\Pi_{12}]} f'_{22}(x^*)$ for some $x^* < \mu\frac{B_0}{2} + \frac{B_1}{2}$.

By concavity of the return functions, the first two cases imply $c^*_{11} > \frac{B_1}{2}$, while the third implies the reverse. Therefore, the project with the higher marginal benefit receives the larger portion of the total budget of resources.

Now consider claim 2. If $\mu_1 = \mu_2$, the optimality condition (3.3) simplifies to $f'_{11}(c_{10})E[\Pi_{11}] - f'_{21}(B_0 - c_{10})E[\Pi_{21}] = 0$. This depends only on period 1, implying a myopic solution in this period. The allocation is myopic also in the last period, since there is no future to account for.

Turning to claim 3 of the proposition, we use the Implicit Function Theorem (IFT). Recall the optimality conditions (3.2) and (3.3) with the optimal quantities $c_{10}(E[\Pi_{12}])$ and $c_{11}(E[\Pi_{12}])$ as functions of the parameter Π_{12}. Using the implicit function theorem to differentiate with respect to $E\Pi_{12}$ yields:

$$\text{from (3.2): } \{f''_{11}(c_{10})E[\Pi_{11}] + f''_{21}(B_0 - c_{10})E[\Pi_{21}]$$

$$+\beta\mu_1(\mu_1 - \mu_2)f''_{12}(\mu_1 c_{10} + c_{11})E[\Pi_{12}]\}\frac{dc_{10}}{dE[\Pi_{12}]}$$

$$+\beta\mu_1(\mu_1 - \mu_2)f''_{12}(\mu_1 c_{10} + c_{11})E[\Pi_{12}]\frac{dc_{11}}{dE[\Pi_{12}]} = -\beta(\mu_1 - \mu_2)f'_{12}(\mu_1 c_{10} + c_{11});$$

$$\text{from (3.3): } \{\mu_1 f''_{12}(\mu_1 c_{10} + c_{11})E[\Pi_{12}] + \mu_2 f''_{22}(\mu_2(B_0 - c_{10}) + B_1 - c_{11})E[\Pi_{22}]\}\frac{dc_{10}}{dE[\Pi_{12}]}$$

$$+\{f''_{12}(\mu_1 c_{10} + c_{11})E[\Pi_{12}] + f''_{22}(\mu_2(B_0 - c_{10}) + B_1 - c_{11})E[\Pi_{22}]\}\frac{dc_{11}}{dE[\Pi_{12}]}$$

$$= -f'_{12}(\mu_1 c_{10} + c_{11}).$$

The quantities c_{10} and c_{11} refer to the optimal points. Solving this system of equations gives $\frac{dc_{10}}{dE[\Pi_{12}]} = \frac{D_{c_{10}/E[\Pi_{12}]}}{D}$, where D is the determinant of the resulting Hessian matrix, and $D_{c_{10}/E[\Pi_{12}]}$ is the determinant for the variable into consideration. The algebra reveals that $D > 0$ is always positive (due to space constraints, we omit the calculations here). Thus, the sign of the first order derivative will depend upon the sign of $D_{c_{10}/E[\Pi_{12}]}$. The value of this determinant is $D_{c_{10}/E[\Pi_{12}]} = -\beta(\mu_1 - \mu_2)$ $f'_{12}(\mu_1 c_{10} + c_{11}) f''_{22}(\mu_2(B_0 - c_{10}) + B_1 - c_{11}) E[\Pi_{22}]$, which implies that:

$$\frac{dc_{10}}{dE[\Pi_{12}]} = \begin{cases} > 0 \text{ if } \mu_1 \geq \mu_2 \\ < 0 \text{ if } \mu_1 < \mu_2 \end{cases}.$$

With similar reasoning (details omitted here), we can show that $\frac{dc_{11}}{dE[\Pi_{12}]} > 0$, and $\frac{dc_{10}}{dE[\Pi_{11}]} > 0$.

We now turn to claim 4 of the proposition. The line of reasoning for the comparative statics $\frac{dc_{10}}{d\mu_1}$ is the same as in claim 3. We omit the detailed calculations; they result in the relationship:

$$\begin{aligned} sign\{\frac{dc_{10}}{d\mu_1}\} = \ & sign\{-\beta f'_{12}(\mu_1 c_{10} + c_{11})E[\Pi_{12}](f''_{12}(\mu_1 c_{10} + c_{11})E[\Pi_{12}] \\ & + f''_{22}(\mu_2(B_0 - c_{10}) + B_1 - c_{11})E[\Pi_{22}]) \\ & - \beta c_{10}(\mu_1 - \mu_2)f''_{12}(\mu_1 c_{10} + c_{11})E[\Pi_{12}]f''_{22}(\mu_2(B_0 - c_{10}) \\ & + B_1 - c_{11})E[\Pi_{22}]\}. \end{aligned}$$

This relationship can be simplified to:

$$\frac{dc_{10}}{d\mu_1} = \begin{cases} \text{positive or negative, if } \mu_1 > \mu_2 \\ > 0 \text{if } \mu_1 \leq \mu_2 \end{cases}.$$

If $\mu_1 > \mu_2$, the sign of $\frac{dc_{10}}{d\mu_1}$ depends on the form of the investment return functions. However, if only one of the two return functions f_{12}, f_{22} is approximately linear, that is, if $f''_{12}(x) \simeq 0$ in the interval $[0, B_0 + B_1]$, we obtain that $\frac{dc_{10}}{d\mu_1} > 0$. The comparison $c_{10}|_{\mu_i > \mu_j} > c_{10}|_{\mu_i = \mu_j}$ results from the first-period optimality condition (3.3) together with concavity of the return functions (varying μ_i and holding μ_j constant).

Turning to claim 5, a simple numerical example shows that for increasing μ_1 (constant μ_2), the total optimal allocation $c_{10}^* + c_{11}^*$ can decrease. Suppose $f_{11}(c) = f_{21}(c) = \frac{c}{c+2}$, $f_{12}(c) = f_{22}(c) = \frac{c}{c+100}$, $= E[\Pi_{11}] = E[\Pi_{21}] = 1000$, and $E[\Pi_{12}] =$

$E[\Pi_{22}] = 1500$. The budgets are $B_0 = 100$, and $B_1 = 150$. Then the total optimal

allocation first increases and then decreases in μ_1:

μ_1	μ_2	c_{10}^*	c_{11}^*	$c_{10}^* + c_{11}^*$
0.12	0.02	58	71	129
0.22	0.02	64	68	132
0.32	0.02	67	64	131
0.42	0.02	70	60	130
0.52	0.02	72	56	128

The 6th and final claim of the proposition concerns the total optimal budget $B_0^* + B_1^*$.

The optimal total budget is the quantity of resources that renders inactive the budget

constraints in both periods: $B_0^* = \widetilde{c_{10}} + \widetilde{c_{20}}$ and $B_1^* = \widetilde{c_{11}} + \widetilde{c_{21}}$. Here, the quantities

$\widetilde{c_{it}}$ are the solutions to the two unconstrained (and thus independent) maximization

problems:

$$\max \left\{ -c_{i0} + \beta f_{i1}(c_{i0})E[\Pi_{i1}] - \beta c_{i1} + \beta^2 f_{i2}(\mu_i c_{i0} + c_{i1})E[\Pi_{i2}] \right\} \quad \text{for every } i.$$

These problems have as optimality conditions:

$$\beta f_{i1}'(c_{i0})E[\Pi_{i1}] - 1 + \beta^2 \mu_i f_{i2}'(\mu_i c_{i0} + c_{i1})E[\Pi_{i2}] = 0 \ \text{(first period)}$$
$$\beta^2 f_{i2}'(\mu_i c_{i0} + c_{i1})E[\Pi_{i2}] - 1 = 0 \ \text{(last period)}$$

The last period optimal budget depends on the carry over effect only through the

optimal resource quantity, using the Implicit Function Theorem:

$$\frac{dB_1^*}{d\mu_i} = \frac{d\widetilde{c_{i1}}}{d\mu_i} = -\frac{\beta^2 f_{i2}''(\mu_i \widetilde{c_{i0}} + \widetilde{c_{i1}})E[\Pi_{i2}]}{(\widetilde{c_{i0}} - \beta f_{i1}''(\widetilde{c_{i0}})E[\Pi_{i1}])\beta^2 f_{i2}''(\mu_i \widetilde{c_{i0}} + \widetilde{c_{i1}})E[\Pi_{i2}]}$$
$$= -\frac{1}{(\widetilde{c_{i0}} - \beta f_{i1}''(\widetilde{c_{i0}})E[\Pi_{i1}])} < 0.$$

The first period optimal budget condition is $\beta f_{i1}'(c_{i0})E[\Pi_{i1}] - 1 + \mu_i = 0$ (after

substituting the second period condition), implying

$$\frac{dB_0^*}{d\mu_i} = \frac{d\widetilde{c_{i0}}}{d\mu_i} = -\frac{\beta f_{i1}''(\widetilde{c_{i0}})E[\Pi_{i1}]}{1} > 0.$$

The total budget change is the sum of these two expressions, which may be positive

or negative. $\square$

Proof of Proposition 3.2. We compare the second period optimality conditions:

$$\frac{f'_{12}(\mu_1^H c_{10} + c_{11}^H)}{f'_{22}(\mu_2(B_0 - c_{10}) + B_1 - c_{11}^H)} = \frac{E[\Pi_{22}]}{E[\Pi_{12}]} = \frac{f'_{12}(\mu_1^L c_{10} + c_{11}^L)}{f'_{22}(\mu_2(B_0 - c_{10}) + B_1 - c_{11}^L)}.$$

Thus, $\mu_1^H > \mu_1 > \mu_1^L$ together with concavity implies $c_{11}^L > c_{11} > c_{11}^H$, or equivalently:

$$f'_{22}(\mu_2(B_0 - c_{10}) + B_1 - c_{11}(\mu_1^H)) < f'_{22}(\mu_2(B_0 - c_{10}) + B_1 - c_{11}(\mu_2)) < f'_{22}(\mu_2(B_0 -$$

$$c_{10}) + B_1 - c_{11}(\mu_1^H)).$$

After observing that $E[\mu_1'] = \mu_1 \Leftrightarrow \mu_1^H p + \mu_1^L (1 - p) = \mu_1$, we rewrite the first

period optimality condition as follows:

$$f'_{11}(c_{10})E[\Pi_{11}] - f'_{21}(B_0 - c_{10})E[\Pi_{21}]$$

$$+\beta p(\mu_1^H - \mu_2)f'_{22}(\mu_2(B_0 - c_{10}) + B_1 - c_{11}^H)E[\Pi_{22}]$$

$$+\beta(1 - p)(\mu_1^L - \mu_2)f'_{22}(\mu_2(B_0 - c_{10}) + B_1 - c_{11}^L)E[\Pi_{22}] = 0. \qquad (3.A.2)$$

But observe that both for μ_1^j $(j = H, L)$

$$(\mu_1^j - \mu_2)f'_{22}(\mu_2(B_0 - c_{10}) + B_{11} - c_{11}^j)E[\Pi_{22}]$$

$$< \quad (\mu_1 - \mu_2)f'_{22}(\mu_2(B_0 - c_{10}) + B_{11} - c_{11})E[\Pi_{22}].$$

Given our assumptions, the carried over marginal benefit of (3.A.2) is smaller than the

equivalent deterministic, which together with concavity of $f_{it}(.)$ implies $c_{10}^* < c_{10}^{\text{det}}$.

□

Proof of Theorem 3.3. The maximization problem (3.4) once we assume that the

budget constraints are tight and binding can be solved by its equivalent Langrangean.

However, before proceeding with the Langrangean, we can utilize the fact that $c_{10} +$

$c_{20} = B_0$, and $c_{11} + c_{21} = B_1$ in order to rewrite the arguments of the functions $f_{it}(.)$.

The arguments now become c_{10} and $(B_0 - c_{10})$ in period 1, and $((\mu_1 - \lambda_2)c_{10} + \lambda_2 B_0 +$

$c_{11}, (\mu_2 - \lambda_1)(B_0 - c_{10}) + \lambda_1 B_0 + B_1 - c_{11})$ in period 2. It is straightforward from

that point that by employing the proposed transformation we get the same problem

as in Theorem 3.2. □

Proof of Theorem 3.4. We maximize the Langrangean

$$L_u(c_{10}, c_{20}, c_{11}, c_{21}) = \max_{\substack{c_{10}, c_{20} \\ c_{11}, c_{21}}} E[u\{(-c_{10} - c_{20}) + \beta\overline{\Pi}_{t=1} + \beta(-c_{11} - c_{21})$$

$$+ \beta^2 \overline{\Pi}_{t=2} + v_0(B_0 - c_{10} - c_{20}) + v_1(B_1 - c_{11} - c_{21})\}]$$

The Kuhn-Tucker conditions are $c_{it}\frac{\partial L_u}{\partial c_{it}} = 0$, $c_{it} \geq 0$, $\frac{\partial L_u}{\partial c_{it}} \geq 0$, $v_j\frac{\partial L_u}{\partial v_j} = 0$, and $\frac{\partial L_u}{\partial v_j} \geq 0$. If both constraints are active (tight budget constraints), i.e. $c_{20} = B_0 - c_{10}$, and $c_{21} = B_1 - c_{11}$, we get conditions (3.5) and (3.6).

We calculate the second order conditions at the first-order condition: $\frac{\partial^2 L_u}{\partial c_{10}^2} < 0$ and det(Hessian) > 0. They can be shown to hold (details are omitted), which proves the result. $\qquad\square$

Proof of Proposition 3.3. By symmetry of the problem, we need to consider only c_{10}^*. The proof follows the same logic as the proof of Proposition 3.1. To prove the first claim, we observe in (3.8) that the third term is positive when $\mu_1 > \mu_2$. Thus,

$$f_{11}'(c_{10})\{E[\Pi_{11}] - a\beta^2 f_{11}(c_{10})Var[\Pi_{11}]\}$$

$$-f_{21}'(B_0 - c_{10})\{E[\Pi_{21}] - a\beta^2 f_{21}(B_0 - c_{10})Var[\Pi_{21}]\} < 0 \text{ and thus:}$$

$$\frac{f_{11}'(c_{10}|_{\mu_1>\mu_2})}{f_{21}'(B_0 - c_{10}|_{\mu_1>\mu_2})} < \frac{E[\Pi_{21}] - a\beta^2 f_{21}(B_0 - c_{10})Var[\Pi_{21}]}{E[\Pi_{11}] - a\beta^2 f_{11}(c_{10})Var[\Pi_{11}]} = \frac{f_{11}'(c_{10}|_{\mu_1=\mu_2})}{f_{21}'(B_0 - c_{10}|_{\mu_1=\mu_2})}.$$

The last inequality in combination with the concavity of the return functions proves the result, $c_{10}|_{\mu_1>\mu_2} > c_{10}|_{\mu_1=\mu_2}$.

To prove the second claim, we need to determine $\frac{dc_{10}^*}{dVar[\Pi_{11}]}$. Define $U_{it} = E[\Pi_{it}] - a\beta^2 f_{it}(.)Var[\Pi_{it}]$. Supress the arguments of the functions wherever the context is clear, and apply the IFT by taking the derivative of (3.7) and (3.8) with respect to $Var[\Pi_{11}]$:

$$\{f_{11}''U_{11} - a\beta^2(f_{11}')^2Var[\Pi_{11}] + f_{21}''U_{21} - a\beta^2(f_{21}')^2Var[\Pi_{21}]$$

$$+ \beta\mu_1(\mu_1 - \mu_2)f_{12}''U_{12} - a\beta^3\mu_1(\mu_1 - \mu_2)(f_{12}')^2Var[\Pi_{12}]\}\frac{dc_{10}^*}{dVar[\Pi_{11}]}$$

$$+ \{\beta(\mu_1 - \mu_2)f_{12}''U_{12} - a\beta^3(\mu_1 - \mu_2)(f_{12}')^2Var[\Pi_{12}]\}\frac{dc_{11}^*}{dVar[\Pi_{11}]} = a\beta^2 f_{11}f_{11}';$$

$$\{\mu_1 f_{12}'' U_{12} - a\beta^2 \mu_1 (f_{12}')^2 Var[\Pi_{12}] + \mu_2 f_{22}'' U_{22} - a\beta^2 \mu_2 (f_{22}')^2 Var[\Pi_{22}]\} \frac{dc_{10}^*}{dVar[\Pi_{11}]}$$

$$+ \{f_{12}'' U_{12} - a\beta^2 (f_{12}')^2 Var[\Pi_{12}] + f_{22}'' U_{22} - a\beta^2 (f_{22}')^2 Var[\Pi_{22}]\} \frac{dc_{11}^*}{dVar[\Pi_{11}]} = 0.$$

The determinant of the system of equations is positive. Hence the sign of $\frac{dc_{10}^*}{dVar[\Pi_{11}]}$ is determined by:

$$\det \begin{bmatrix} a\beta^2 f_{11} f_{11}' & \beta(\mu_1 - \mu_2) f_{12}'' U_{12} - a\beta^3 (\mu_1 - \mu_2)(f_{12}')^2 Var[\Pi_{12}] \\ 0 & f_{12}'' U_{12} - a\beta^2 (f_{12}')^2 Var[\Pi_{12}] + f_{22}'' U_{22} - a\beta^2 (f_{22}')^2 Var[\Pi_{22}] \end{bmatrix} < 0.$$

which is always negative. Hence, $\frac{dc_{10}^*}{dVar[\Pi_{11}]} < 0$.

The proof of the third claim follows the same logical steps as the second. The system of equations, now, has the same LHS but the RHS change to $a\beta^3(\mu_1 - \mu_2) f_{12} f_{12}'$ and $a\beta^2 f_{12} f_{12}'$ respectively. The equivalent determinant becomes $a\beta^3(\mu_1 - \mu_2) f_{12} f_{12}' \{f_{22}'' U_{22} - a\beta^2 (f_{22}')^2 Var[\Pi_{22}]\}$, and the sign depends upon the sign of the carry over effect difference $\mu_1 - \mu_2$. Therefore, we get:

$$\frac{dc_{10}^*}{dVar[\Pi_{12}]} = \{> 0 \text{ if } \mu_1 < \mu_2; \quad = 0 \text{ if } \mu_1 = \mu_2; \quad < 0 \text{ if } \mu_1 > \mu_2\}.$$

Proof of Proposition 3.4. Without loss of generality, take $i = 1$. For simplicity of exposition, we analyze the two cases separately, first a correlation in the first period only. Re-derive the optimality conditions analogously to Proposition 3.2. Then apply the IFT to get take the derivative of c_{10}^* with respect to $Cov[\Pi_{11}, \Pi_{21}]$:

$$sign\{\frac{dc_{10}^*}{dCov[\Pi_{11}, \Pi_{21}]}\}$$
$$= sign\{a\beta^2 (f_{11}'(.) f_{21}(.) - f_{11}(.) f_{21}'(.))$$
$$(f_{12}''(.) U_{12} - a\beta^2 f_{12}'(.) Var[\Pi_{12}] + f_{12}''(.) U_{12} - a\beta^2 f_{12}'(.) Var[\Pi_{12}])\}.$$

The sign of this expression depends on the sign of $f_{11}'(.) f_{21}(.) - f_{11}(.) f_{21}'(.)$. This last term is the marginal gain or loss from investing slightly more on product line 1 starting from the optimal allocation as determined by the optimality conditions. Hence,

$$\frac{dc_{10}^*}{dCov[\Pi_{11}, \Pi_{21}]} = \begin{cases} > 0, \text{ if } f_{11}'(.) f_{21}(.) - f_{11}(.) f_{21}'(.) < 0 \\ < 0, \text{ if } f_{11}'(.) f_{21}(.) - f_{11}(.) f_{21}'(.) > 0 \end{cases}.$$

Repeating the same derivation for the second-period correlation (details omitted), we get:

$$\frac{dc_{10}^{*}}{dCov[\Pi_{12}, \Pi_{22}]} = \{> 0 \text{ if } \mu_1 < \mu_2; \ = 0 \text{ if } \mu_1 = \mu_2; \ < 0 \text{ if } \mu_1 > \mu_2\}.$$

□

Proof of Theorem 3.5. The proof for n product lines and T periods follows the same steps as the proof of Theorem 3.2. It easily verifiable that once all constraints are binding, the common Langrangean multiplier drives the results. The interior point solution is a maximum (if it exists, i.e. the set of equations has a solution). If a solution does not exist, a subset of projects has higher marginal benefits than the others everywhere and the analysis has to be redone for that subset. To see that the FOC is a local maximum assume that we deviate from the optimal solution by increasing c_{it} by $\delta > 0$, and decreasing c_{jt} by δ (corresponding to the tight budget constraint). Call the optimal point slope from (3.10) s (3.10) implies that the slopes with respect to the two different allocations are the same. Now, concavity implies that an increase of c_{it} by δ will contribute less than δs, while the equivalent decrease of c_{jt} by δ reduces the portfolio value by more than δs. Hence, the interior point is a local maximum. The local maximum is also the only global maximum because of the monotonicity of the first order derivative functions.

In order to determine the t period marginal benefit equation, we proceed inductively. For $T = 2$ the result is given by equations similar to Theorem 3.2. Assume that the result holds for t periods. Then, for $t + 1$ periods, the same result follows by rearranging the terms of the obtained summation terms and observing that the resulting terms

$$\mu_i^k - \mu_i^{k-2}\mu_n(\mu_i - \mu_n) - \mu_i^{k-3}\mu_n(\mu_i - \mu_n) - \dots - \mu_i\mu_n^{k-1}(\mu_i - \mu_n) - \mu_n^k = \mu_i^{k-1}(\mu_i - \mu_n)$$

in case the carry-over effects are constant throughout the horizon. Thus,

$$[\prod_{\nu=2}^{k} \mu_{2\nu}]\mu_{2(k+1)}[\prod_{v=k+2}^{T} \mu_{1v}], \text{ and } [\prod_{\nu=2}^{k} \mu_{2\nu}]\mu_{1(k+1)}[\prod_{v=k+2}^{T} \mu_{1v}]$$

cancel out for adjacent values of k in the more general case of time dependent carry-over effects.

□

Chapter 4

APPLYING THE PROJECT SELECTION THEORY AT GEMSTONE

1. Introduction

This chapter reports on an application of the theoretical findings from Chapter 3 in a real world scenario. The study was conducted based on our collaboration with the manager of applied research at GemStone, a medium-sized diamond producer. The idea behind the study[1] was to develop a quantitative portfolio prioritization method for research projects. The department conducts applied process R&D to improve and advance diamond identification, extraction, and processing technologies, with the goal of providing GemStone with lower cost and higher yield operations.

Although the specifics of the problem and the data relate to the host organization, the result of the study is a generally applicable project selection method. We develop a simple *linearized* analysis, which acknowledges the typical difficulty of estimating exact return functions in R&D departments by using easier to estimate linear returns. This allows

---

[1]The name of the company and all numbers are disguised to preserve confidentiality (see Loch and Kavadias 2000).

us to represent the choice procedure in a one-step graphical form, which is now used by GemStone. Based on theoretical insights from Chapter 3, this study provides an example of how theoretical research in Operations Management can be applied to a real setting.

The chapter is organized as follows: after first presenting the host organization, GemStone, we justify the linear selection procedure (Section 3.1 explains the theoretical background, Section 3.2 the data collection, and Section 3.3 the results of the linearized analysis). We conclude (Section 3.4) with a description of what GemStone implemented and with some general insights from the study.

2.   The Diamond Producer GemStone Inc.

2.1   History and Background

GemStone was founded in the 1950s as a small producer of diamonds during a period when new players were emerging in the world diamond industry. GemStone began operating in Northern Canada, and during the 1970s, added interests in Chile and Zaire.

GemStone concentrated on gems (made into jewelry as opposed to industrial diamonds), but did not market its stones to the end consumer. The company sold its entire raw diamond production to the Central Selling Office (CSO), the diamond syndicate in London. The CSO had built a powerful worldwide marketing machine, which emphasized the emotional value and the investment value of diamonds. GemStone was a small player and, as such, had no chance of entering the end consumer market on its own. They therefore performed no direct marketing. Instead, the company effectively sold a commodity product, the quality of which was measured by the "four Cs": carats (weight), color, clarity and cuttability.

Diamonds are formed out of carbon that has been subjected to extremely high pressure and heat. In the early days of diamond mining, until the 1860s, gems had been washed out from surface deposits. But these easily exploited sources were soon exhausted. Today, diamonds are mined from eroded kimberlite pipes, formations of crushed rocks shaped like ice-cream cones that volcanic activity has thrust to the earth's surface from depths that can exceed 150 km. Mining is very capital-intensive – typically, over 1,000 tons of rock have to be excavated and processed in order to extract 100 grams of diamonds of sufficient size and quality. Of the several thousand kimberlite occurrences known in 1990, only about 50 are considered commercially viable.

GemStone's organization reflected the principal activities of producing raw diamonds (top of Figure 4.1) and was structured along the steps of the diamond production process. The exploration team performed aerial photographic surveys and had teams of geologists in the field, who collected rock samples from geologically promising ground formations to identify kimberlite deposits. The ore evaluation group's role was to estimate the richness and the grade of the identified deposits, and to translate these data into a "value estimate" for the potential mine.

Recovery, or "liberation", traditionally happened by crushing the rocks into small sizes, and passing the rock fragments on a conveyor in front of personnel who picked out the diamonds by visual inspection. In this process, a balance had to be struck in the size to which the rocks were crushed. If the rocks remained too large, diamonds remained hidden in them and were overlooked. If crushing was too fine, large diamonds were damaged or even destroyed. Since the value of a gem grew

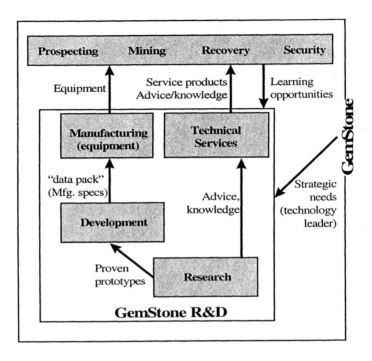

Figure 4.1.   GemStone's Corporate and R&D Structure

steeply with size, one tended to err toward larger rocks. In addition, large gems represented an almost irresistible temptation for inspection personnel. Tight security systems had been installed to prevent theft. One manager estimated that 10-20% of value was lost due to wastage, damage or theft.

The mines were supported by three engineering staff groups (metallurgy, mining, chemical/mechanical processing), who set operating standards, performed audits on single process steps, provided the mines with technical expertise in improving their processes, and looked for "best practice" processes outside of GemStone.

2.2 The Role of R&D at GemStone

R&D had traditionally developed new liberation equipment as well as engineering services both for mining operations and the engineering staff groups. R&D's mission was to "actively create new knowledge and embodiment of new technologies, with delivery on a continuous basis, short and long term, with significant returns." R&D consisted of four units (bottom of Figure 4.1). Manufacturing produced newly developed equipment, from unique one-off machines to small series (up to about 50 units). They built the equipment based on "data packs," or detailed manufacturing specifications, that came from the second group, product development. This product development group had the responsibility of developing new equipment based on new technologies delivered to them by research in the form of working prototypes.

The Research department had two responsibilities: first, developing new technologies with fundamental performance advances which could benefit the operating groups and second, providing deep technical expertise to the technical services organization within R&D. Technical Services supported both the mines and the engineering groups with process improvements, trouble shooting, and efficiency audits, but relied on the research personnel for help with highly complex trouble shooting problems.

During the year 2000, the research department of GemStone had developed a performance measurement system to align their R&D targets with their strategic objectives (described in Loch and Tapper 2002 and in Section 4 of Chapter 2 of this book). One outcome of this exercise was the identification of three strategic activity areas: knowledge creation, support of technical services, and next generation technology development. Technology development was divided into eight areas of technical focus, summarized in Figure 4.2, each headed by a Research Program Manager (RPM).

Areas of expertise	Description
Recovery Technology	*Development of equipment for the location of the diamonds within the ore body and the assessment of their value*
Environmental Technologies	*Examination of the feasibility of conducting the mining operations with environmentally "friendlier" processes*
Sorting Technologies	*Development of processes to separate gem stones from the ore body*
Mining Technologies	*Research on new methods of efficient mining under different soil conditions (e.g., under sea mining and arctic mining)*
Process Optimization	*Automation and optimization of plant operations (referring to the plants operating close to the mines)*
Machine Intelligence	*Research on artificial intelligence methods for anti-theft usage (i.e., gem stone security) and labor security (i.e., accident prevention)*

Figure 4.2. Areas of Expertise in the Research Function

But this left open the question of project prioritization. In the past, projects had been selected by the research manager and the leading experts (research program managers – RPMs) based on experience and personal judgment, which made selection engineering-driven. There had been no formal process in place to ensure a transparent project portfolio selection. While a few innovative projects had been initiated by the explorative spirit of researchers, the operating divisions ("customers") expressed frustration with poorly functioning products, that did not address their main needs. The research department had been perceived by some operating divisions as "disconnected from the real world." Research management was fully aware of the problem, and initiated a portfolio prioritization initiative in 2001. It aimed to enable a quantitative prioritization of the projects in the next generation technology sub-portfolio (technical services were evaluated by operational efficiency numbers, while the less tangible knowledge creation efforts had a separate budget).

3. Selecting the Portfolio at GemStone

This section describes the selection process that was undertaken at GemStone. We explain first the theoretical basis of our selection method and the optimality conditions, and then present the data collection process and the results of the analysis.

3.1 The Selection Method

In Chapter 3, we showed that it is optimal to allocate a scarce budget according to marginal benefits (accounting for multiple periods), as long as the one-period return functions are concave all the way from a zero investment.[2] In other words, it is optimal to simply and intuitively allocate the R&D budget, dollar for dollar, to the project with the highest marginal payoff (accounting for the effect of multiple periods).

In practice, multi-period portfolios (with future resource constraint interactions) are not feasible because they are too complex (see Chapter 2). Rather, both theoretical work and management practice have concentrated on a *de facto* one-period analysis. However, this requires that important future projects, that are already visible today, be taken into

---

[2]The setting in Chapter 3 refers to strategic *programs* at a more aggregate level; programs can often be drastically reduced without losing viability.

account (e.g., an important project to start next year may crowd out a project considered today because of the capacity limits next year).[3]

Research managers found it impossible to estimate the shape of the project return functions for each of the future periods – they simply did not have enough information. However, the multi-period problem can be collapsed into a one-period problem, in which each project's uncertain future payoffs are represented in a decision tree, in isolation of the other projects (e.g., Hess 1993). This collapse into one period is justified because in our setting, projects, once started, no longer compete with one another for resources. In other words, management does not halt successfully ongoing projects for budget reasons – a project will be allowed to continue as long as it progresses well. It is common practice in R&D management that ongoing projects are usually stopped only when they yield bad results,[4] and not for budget reasons. Re-prioritization because of budget cuts is the exception, and typically constitutes a traumatic and unforeseen experience for an R&D organization for reasons that lie outside the scope of a quantitative optimization model (such as loss of credibility or demoralization). GemStone management did not stop well progressing projects, unless there was a policy of severe cost cutting, which was not foreseen at the time of the study. This attitude is justified under (a) the absence of radical budget cuts in the near future, and (b) the absence of a highly promising future project, the imminent start of which management is already aware. If such a "star waiting in the wings" existed, it might crowd out a currently started project in the

---

[3]The projects started now should not exceed the capacity of future periods. This point is, however, tricky, if projects have significant cancellation probabilities; in this case, the pipeline should be "speculatively" overloaded so as not yo underutilize future capacity. See Ding and Eliashberg 2002.

[4]And perhaps not even then, see Boulding *et al.* 1997, and Schmidt and Calantone 1998. The assumption that projects, once started, are not cancelled for budget reasons also underlies the well-known knapsack models of constrained optimization.

next period. Thus, management should already be considering such a project now.

Managers often do consider future contingencies at the project level, for example, using a decision tree structure to capture the additional value of managerial flexibility (real options). Real options increase project value[5] (e.g., Newton and Pearson 1994; Trigeorgis 1996; Luehrman 1998; Loch and Bode-Greuel 2001). This was also done at GemStone, representing projects as decision trees (as in Figure 4.3).

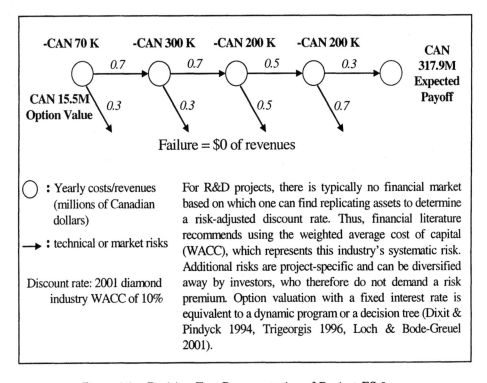

Figure 4.3. Decision Tree Representation of Project ES-2

The validity of this simplification is summarized in Decision Result 1 (the proofs of all decision results are included in the Appendix).

---

[5]In contrast to previously dominant valuation methods, such as net present value (NPV, see Hess 1993; Sharpe and Kellin 1998), or break even times (BET, see House and Price 1991).

Decision Result 1: *If a project, once approved, is never canceled for budget reasons (only if it performs badly), the dynamic portfolio selection problem (over multiple periods) can be simplified to a choice of single-period projects competing for budget funding. Each of the projects is characterized by its first-year resource requirements and its option value at the end of that year.*

The R&D *program* theory of Chapter 3 must be modified because *project* funding cannot be reduced all the way down to zero without losing the project's viability. A project budget can be reduced only within certain limits – measures, such as intensifying resource utilization, or excluding redundant but costly features of the end product, work only up to a point (e.g., Meyer and Utterback 1995; Bayus 1997; Kessler and Bierly 2002). Below a certain minimum, a project is often not viable (this is graphically shown in Figure 4.3). The fact that budget increases at some point cease to produce additional benefits (see Brooks 1975) does not pose a problem for the theory of Chapter 3 because a return function that is flat above a certain investment level is concave.

GemStone's projects have, thus, feasibility limits (c_{down} and c_{up}), between which the project return function is concave (exhibits decreasing returns). This is consistent with the research managers' intuition. The problem is that a lower feasibility limit may invalidate the marginal benefit logic: suppose that the project with the highest marginal benefit uses so many resources that no additional project fits into the budget. Then, two other projects may exist, each with a lower marginal value, but combined, they fully use the existing budget capacity, and thus generate a higher total value than if the highest margin project is funded alone (wasting part of the budget). This is, of course, exactly the reason why optimal R&D budget allocation is usually approached with Mathematical Programming (MP) methods.

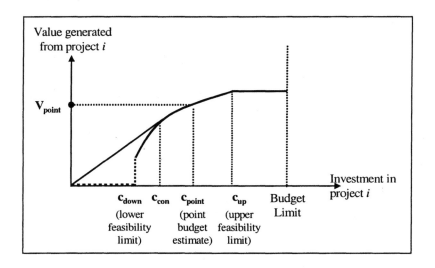

Figure 4.4. Qualitative Form of Project Return Functions

However, we can still avoid MP under a reasonable approximation. Draw a line from the origin that touches the return function in the feasible region, a point which we call c_{con} (allocation must start from zero because otherwise, marginal benefits carry no information about the total project return). Along this line, the marginal benefit is constant, and thus, the project might as well get an investment of c_{con} if it gets any investment at all (see Figure 4.3).[6]

---

[6]Between c_{down} and c_{con}, the approximated function overstates the total project benefit, but it understates the marginal benefit, so the allocation procedure works correctly. This approximation, *concavification*, is used in Finance theory to approximate S-shaped utility curves. Moreover, as we linearize the return functions, the marginal benefit is constant.

We can then find an intuitive allocation that gives each dollar to the project with the highest return for that dollar at that point. In general, project return functions are non-linear (as shown in Figure 4.3). However, their estimation is often very difficult, due to uncertainty and the lack of data on comparable projects. That is, the inaccuracies of estimating non-linear return functions may outweigh the benefits of non-linear data for the value of the optimal portfolio (see Section 3.2 below). This is particularly the case if the return functions are quite flat (if returns are only mildly decreasing), or if the feasibility ranges of the projects are narrow. Therefore, we approximate the project return functions by linear functions (straight lines in Figure 4.3).[7] In this case, we can formulate a very simple and intuitive decision procedure:

Decision Result 2: *If the projects have* **constant marginal returns** *within their feasibility limits (a project i offers a payoff of r_i for each additional dollar of investment), projects are prioritized as follows: rank the projects according to their marginal returns r_i. Resources are always allocated to the highest-ranked project up to its upper feasibility limit, and then to the next, etc., until the budget is exhausted.*

If the nth project no longer fits into the budget, the allocation is adjusted in one of two ways: (a) the allocations of the projects that were fitted into the budget last are successively reduced (if necessary, down to their respective lower limits) until the nth projects fits into the budget. The value of this portfolio is compared to the value of the original portfolio (without project n), and the better one is chosen.

---

[7]An analysis of the more general case of non-linear concave return functions, as well as an example of their estimation, is given in Kavadias *et al.* 2003.

(b) the total budget is increased by the amount necessary to fit in the nth project (this will be realistic only if the necessary budget increase is very small and can be justified by making an entire project feasible). □

We prove optimality of this procedure in the Appendix. This linearized procedure not only requires fewer data (only linear return estimates per dollar invested), but it can be performed *during the decision meeting*: armed with the returns of each project, the management team can create the ranking on real time, and infuse it with managerial judgment of additional (possibly intangible) considerations.

In fact, the linearized procedure corresponds to something managers have long been doing anyway: rank projects according to their Return on Investment (ROI). Thus, our result confirms that this longstanding method indeed makes sense, *provided* that the decision makers are aware that this requires them to shuffle resources or to stretch the total budget such that the projects can fill the budget perfectly (that no budget goes wasted). It is this proviso that eliminates the need for more complex MP methods.

3.2 Collecting the Project Data

The technology development sub-portfolio had been assigned a budget of CAN 1.775 million (Canadian dollars) for the year 2001. The first part of data collection required us to estimate the project return and budget, V_{point} and c_{point}.

In cooperation with the eight RPMs, we collected estimations of the following variables: (a) **Annual costs per project**. The major cost component was manpower, about which the RPMs could usually make reasonable estimates. (b) **Technical and market risks**, estimated as the probability that a project currently under development would continue to receive resources in the following year, and (c) **Projected rewards** of the resulting technology implementations after launch. Again, yearly point estimates were provided. Whereas costs were usually easy to obtain, market values required collaboration and discussion between R&D management and its customers, the operating mines. Risks reflected the potential of the project to reach the final stage and be successfully launched in the market. We defined these risks as stage-gate probabilities: "the probability that a project that has come thus far, continues to the next phase."[8]

The collected data were iterated twice to (a) obtain the best possible estimates, and (b) determine whether resource requirements could be adjusted up or down. The RPMs had to contact their internal customers, such as mine engineers, and *explore* the potential benefits of their technologies in the field. The projected rewards had to be agreed upon by the RPMs (as suppliers) and the mines (as customers). Finally, the possible adjustments, which yielded the return functions, were derived through discussions among the RPMs and the authors. The RPMs were given possible investment amounts (as percentages of the point estimates of the resource requirements), and were asked to approximately assess the output value generated. In the course of the data collection, the project characterizations were repeatedly discussed among the RPMs, the research manager, and the authors.

The authors carefully explained the selection procedure to the RPMs, in order to acquire homogeneous data estimates. For example, RPMs

---

[8]The major risks were failure and cancellation. In other contexts, risks may include contingencies that require changes of the project plan or target market segments. This makes the decision tree more complex, but the basic approach remains the same (Loch and Bode-Greuel 2001).

conceptualized success probabilities differently – some viewed them as transition probabilities (chance of continuing from one year to the next), while others had in mind the risk profile of the project (probability of the project being successful overall). Figure 4.5 provides a summary of the current project portfolio, with the point estimates for the project resource requirements and option values (the roots of the decision trees in Figure 4.3).[9]

Project Name	Technological Area	Cost (CAN)	Expected Value (CAN)
ES-1	Recovery	0.25	0.51
ES-2	Recovery	0.07	15.58
Valuation Technologies	Recovery	0.06	16.62
ET-1	Environmental	0.27	5.92
Processing Technologies	Environmental	0.2	15.30
HT Recovery	Sorting	0.16	7.37
MC	Sorting	0.036	6.1
MGS	Sorting	0.07	4.98
Process Optimisation	Process Optimization	0.7	22.41
DCH	Mining	0.15	12.87
ElSuP	Machine Intelligence	0.15	2.58

Figure 4.5. Overview of Candidate Projects

The summary of the data reveals a wide range of ROI in the research portfolio. A simple addition of the third column of Figure 5.5 shows that the sum of the costs of the projects currently in the portfolio was higher

---

[9]The full multi-period trees for all projects are available by the authors.

than the total budget. In the past, no explicit prioritization process had existed, and when technology level projects needed more money, they just took it from the knowledge-building budget, potentially crowding out long-term breakthrough ideas.

The second part of data estimation was concerned with the return functions and budget limits. The RPMs agreed that all projects had decreasing returns (as in Figure 4.3) – adding to a project's budget would increase its payoff less than taking away from the budget would reduce it. However, they believed the return functions were quite flat (close to linear), and estimating the curvature was very difficult (see Kavadias *et al.* 2003). The feasible budget variation, in contrast, could be estimated: although each project was slightly different, the RPMs felt that a variation up and down by 10% from the point estimate c_{point} was approximately the feasible range for all projects.

Here, we report only on the data collection for the linear analysis that was ultimately used by GemStone. The final estimations were fed back to the RPMs and the research manager, to validate whether they were perceived as realistic.

3.3   Selecting the Portfolio With Linear Returns

Figure 4.6 summarizes the analysis. The portfolio value curve includes the projects in the order of their linearized marginal returns (value per dollar invested, as calculated from the point values in Figure 4.5). The allocation funds all projects to the full upper limit of their resource requirements (110%), in the order of decreasing marginal returns until the budget is exhausted. The value from the higher investment is simply linearly extrapolated to the upper feasibility limit.

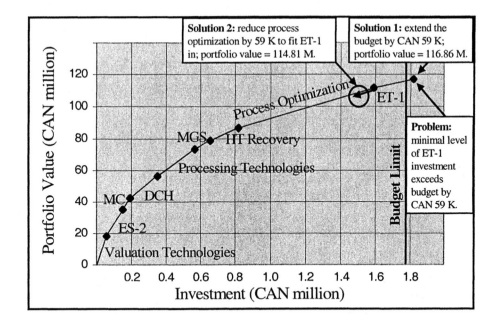

Figure 4.6. Optimal Portfolio with Linear Returns

Then the question is what to do with the last project, ET-1. Its lower feasible investment (at 90%) does not fit in the budget, and less investment would be a waste (the project would not be viable). Figure 4.6 shows two strategies: either the budget is increased by 3.3% (CAN 59 K) to fit ET-1 in, or the budget of the least attractive project so far included (Process Optimization) is reduced to allow ET-1 to fit in the budget. Obviously, the former strategy has a higher total value (CAN 116.68 versus 114.81 million), but now, management can decide whether they want to make the additional investment to obtain that additional value. What is important is that the value curve in Figure 4.6 offers a powerful visualization tool that GemStone management appreciates. Moreover, the solution offered by this simple tool is indeed optimal (and much better, in this case, than the optimal MP solution that does not allow for adjustments in the project allocations – it would yield only CAN 107.2 million because it would leave CAN 60 K of the available budget unused). The reason for the simpler tool giving a better solution lies in the acknowledgment that project investments can be varied.

In comparison to a full analysis with exact non-linear returns, the set of supported projects is slightly different. However, the set of projects for which the two analyses disagree comprises precisely the "borderline" projects, for which the decision might go either way. Therefore, the error is unlikely to be large.

At the end of the study, the research manager concluded that the effort of collecting the decreasing returns data was not justified by increased accuracy, especially since it could not be done exactly. However, he was encouraged by the simplicity and power of the linearized allocation procedure: "It gives us confidence to do something that we sort of have done intuitively, namely ranking the projects by their ROI. Shifting project budgets also comes natural to us, and now, after having done this study, we can do it explicitly to maximize value."

4.   Discussion and Conclusion

Quantitative methods, such as MP, have not found widespread application in R&D portfolio selection because they are complex and hard to use. The disconnect partly stems from the assumption that projects must be either "in" or "out" of the portfolio, which causes combinatorial complexity of the methods. In practice, however, budgets can be adjusted up or down (our host manager stated, "there is no project that can not have its resources varied"). Explicitly taking this into account, we developed a portfolio selection method for the technology development projects of the applied research group of GemStone, a medium-sized diamond producer.

As is usual in R&D portfolio literature and practice, we focus the analysis on a one-period problem by collapsing multi-period projects into an NPV (the root of a decision tree). Once project budget variation is allowed, projects may be prioritized by a "value per dollar of budget investment", or their *marginal benefits*. Due to the limited precision of data estimation (which is typical for R&D environments), we treat the project returns as if they were linear.

Our procedure simply ranks the projects according to their value per dollar invested, and fully fund (up to the feasibility limit) the most attractive projects until the budget is exhausted. If the last project does not fit exactly, one can either extend the budget a bit to fit the project in, or shift resources from the least attractive project included before. This simple linear method may not only be just as accurate as more complex methods, since available data are notoriously imprecise in an R&D context, it can also be implemented in one step in an easily understood and constructed graph (even within the decision meeting).

While the "success" of the chosen portfolio at GemStone will not be known for a few more years, the organization has made several process changes based on this project. The research manager had confidence in the findings because he could relate the result of the study to a method that he knew before – ranking projects by their ROI. First, his group adopted the decision tree representation of projects (Figure 4.3) to produce the point value estimation in a high quality and transparent manner. Second, the group has begun to consider the effect of project budget variations, namely cut-backs to accommodate additional projects and the benefit of accelerating high value projects with additional resources.

Third, prioritization has now taken hold in management thinking – as the manager stated, "In the past, we were bullied into accepting all high value projects, whether we had the resources to do them or not. This resulted in unhappiness because of slow progress. We are better at saying 'no' now, and we can support it by the logic of project viability below a certain budget investment." The research controller is now committed to introduce the linear valuation tool (Figure 4.6) across the board, and the Vice President of overall R&D supports this effort.

A "side effect" was that the research department has since intensified its communication with its internal customers to improve data reliability and increase the customers' involvement and commitment. On the other hand, this has caused unhappiness from Exploration: they feel the quantitative approach to project prioritization is unfavorable to them as their project benefits are more difficult to quantify. This shows that a dynamic of striving for better numbers has taken effect, and the tension forces the groups to address the varying estimation errors in the numbers. As for any quantitative method, prioritization methods should not only (perhaps not even primarily) provide "answers", but foster transparency, understanding, and discussion.

APPENDIX 4.A

Decision Result 1. Suppose I is the set of n candidate projects for the portfolio. The discount factor is β, project i's period t development cost is c_{it}, and the final payoff Π_i. The transition probabilities of "successful progress and thus continuation" are p_{it}, and the probabilities of termination $(1 - p_{it})$. They are independent, thus $Pr\{i$ and j move successfully to t+1$\} = p_{it}p_{jt}$. Then, the optimal portfolio is the solution to the problem

$$V_t(I) = \max_{J \subseteq I}\{-\sum_{j \in J} c_{jt} + \beta \sum_{K \subseteq J} \Pr\{K \mid J\}V_{t+1}(K)\}, \text{ subject to } \sum_{j \in J} c_{jt} \leq B_t. \quad (4.A.1)$$

$V_{t+1}(K)$ is the dynamic programming value function of the set K of projects pursued in period $t + 1$. $\Pr\{K \mid J\}$ is the probability that a subset K of the chosen set J of projects will successfully continue into period $t + 1$. (4.A.1) optimizes the selection over all possible realizations, given the budget constraints in each period.

Result 1 states that we include the n best candidates in terms of their individual dynamic programming value function V_j, once we have no budget constraints in the future. That is, the optimal portfolio is given by:

$$\max_{J \subseteq I}\{-\sum_{j \in J} c_{j1} + \beta \sum_{j \in J} p_{j1}V_j\}, \text{ subject to } \sum_{j \in J} c_{j1} \leq B_1. \quad (4.A.2)$$

Proof of Result 1. We prove the result for 2-period projects. For more periods, the argument is applied repetitively. From (4.A.1) we get:

$$V_1(I) = \max_{J \subseteq I}\{-\sum_{j \in J} c_{j1} + \beta \sum_{K \subseteq J} \Pr\{K \mid J\} \max_{L \subseteq K}\{-\sum_{l \in L} c_{l2} + \beta \sum_{M \subseteq L} \Pr\{M \mid L\}V_3(M)\}\}$$

subject to $\sum_{j \in J} c_{j1} \leq B_1$, and $\sum_{l \in L} c_{l2} \leq B_2$. By the funding guarantee condition, we remove the budget constraint in the second period. Therefore, the problem simplifies to:

$$V_1(I) = \max_{J \subseteq I}\{-\sum_{j \in J} c_{j1} + \beta \sum_{K \subseteq J} \Pr\{K \mid J\}(-\sum_{k \in K} c_{k2} + \beta \sum_{L \subseteq K} \Pr\{L \mid K\}V_3(L))\}$$

subject to $\sum_{j \in J} c_{j1} \leq B_1$. The last part of the maximization term can be written as:

$$V_2(K) = -\sum_{k \in K} c_{k2} + \beta \sum_{L \subseteq K} \Pr\{L \mid K\}V_3(L).$$

As we know that the projects are independent and $\Pr\{L \mid K\} = \prod_{k \in L} p_{k2} \prod_{k \in K \setminus L}(1 - p_{k2})$, we can write:

$$\sum_{L \subseteq K} \Pr\{L \mid K\}V_3(L) = \sum_{k \in K} V_k(\sum_{L \subseteq K, \, k \in L} \Pr\{L \mid K\}) = \sum_{k \in K} p_{k2}V_k.$$

The first period problem (after translating the $\Pr\{J \mid K\}$ analogously) becomes (4.A.2).   □

Proof of Decision Result 2. As long as the budget is not exhausted, a simple exchange argument shows that adding the projects with the highest returns first must be optimal. It is the budget constraint that represents the complication. The proof is concerned with part (a) of the result (it is clear that part (b), increasing the budget limit, yields a higher total return – this is a political challenge, not a question of optimality).

If project n is added, again an exchange argument shows that the project whose allocation should be reduced is the one with the lowest return, or the one that was added to the portfolio last. This minimizes the loss from reducing an allocation. When this project has reached its lower feasibility limit, the next-to-last project's allocation should be reduced, and so on, until project n fits into the budget. Thus, we end up with two candidate solutions: either leave project n out, or fit it in by freeing up sufficient budget in the way described above.

Say, in fitting in project n, k projects have had their allocations reduced by Δc_i, $i = 1, \cdots, k$. The total portfolio value change from fitting in project n is then:

$$\Delta V = r_n c_{down}(n) - \sum_{i=1}^{k} r_i \Delta c_i. \qquad (4.\text{A}.3)$$

As $r_i \geq r_n$ for all i, this value change is positive only if enough capacity is "recuperated" by adding project n, that is, if $c_{down}(n)$ exceeds $\sum_{i=1}^{k} \Delta c_i$ sufficiently to make up for the lower return on the capacity that was freed by the other k projects. This is the comparison in Decision Result 2, which is shown in Figure 4.6.   □

Chapter 5

ADMITTING PROJECTS ONE-BY-ONE AS THEY ARRIVE

1.   Introduction

This chapter[1] addresses the portfolio selection problem when project decisions must be taken one-by-one. Most research on project selection and resource allocation views portfolio choices as low-frequency (e.g., quarterly or annually) decisions that prioritize among multiple projects or product lines.

While this line of research addresses important strategic decisions, it neglects the irregular timing of new potential development ideas and the associated lack of synchronicity in the decision process. Project proposals do not arise as a neat portfolio in time for the annual review, but often one-by-one at unpredictable points in time, and decisions about them must often be taken quickly (if not for funding, then a pre-screening for an inclusion into the annual portfolio review). In the

---

[1]This chapter has benefited from Svenja Sommer's comments at INSEAD

words of Gemstone's research manager (see Chapter 4), "We do have an annual portfolio review, but that's not enough when projects come one by one. While there is a general assessment of whether a project fits our strategic priorities, at this point, it comes down to seeing whether we have the capabilities to do it and whether it is attractive enough."

This problem represents, in the language of queueing or processing systems, an *admission control* problem: as project ideas are generated, which ones should be accepted and which ones rejected? In this chapter, we derive an optimal admission policy for projects of varying potential reward that "arrive" at unpredictable points in time.

We find that project acceptance in the portfolio is determined by a threshold: If the project payoff is above the threshold, allocate resources to the project. The threshold decreases with the currently available capacity: more free capacity prompts the organization the be less choosy in admitting ideas. This is intuitive, but difficult to show in a model in closed form.

The chapter is organized as follows: Section 2 introduces the stylized model, and Section 3 presents the optimal admission policy. We discuss the managerial implications in Section 4.

2.   Model Setup

Like Lewis *et al.* 1999, we model the product development organization as an $M/M/N$ processing system. A set of N servers can process projects (one each) in parallel. All servers are symmetric in their capability to process a project, and their total number provides a surrogate metric for the development capacity of the organization.

"Project-generating" ideas arrive stochastically, according to a Poisson process of rate λ (on average, every $\frac{1}{\lambda}$ time units a new project idea arrives). Each idea, once noticed, is analyzed with respect to its attractiveness (for example, ROI or NPV or market share). The attractiveness is captured by a "payoff" denoted by Π. This is a continuous non-negative random variable with a cumulative distribution $F(\Pi)$ of known mean $\overline{\Pi}$ and variance σ_{Π}^2 (both finite).[2] We assume that all projects have, *a priori*, the same exponential distribution of development time (resource requirements) with mean $1/\mu$ (this can be interpreted as all projects being of the same overall category). Moreover, we assume that the development cost is a function of the service time. Without loss of generality, we normalize the costs to zero, since all servers are symmetric. The entire system is an $M/M/N$ queue with admission control.

The product development manager decides dynamically whether to include the newly arrived idea of payoff Π in the current portfolio of active projects. We consider only Markov decision policies $\delta(n, \Pi)$ that depend on the number of open capacity slots (development servers) and the payoff of the current project (previous decisions are sunk). Once an

---

[2]To avoid unnecessary technicalities, we assume that the support of $F(x)$ is an interval of the form (Π_{lower}, ∞) with $\Pi_{lower} > 0$, since organizations rarely consider projects that have 0 payoff.

idea is admitted in the portfolio, it immediately starts to receive service from one of the available servers.

A rejected idea can stay around and be reconsidered in case of the state of the available capacity.[3] However, rejected ideas soon become obsolete (which is again common in NPD organizations). We model this with a waiting buffer of capacity one, from which the currently waiting idea is pushed out by a newly arriving idea independently of the payoff:[4] the newer and fresher idea supplants the previous one. Finally, time affects the project value through a discount rate β ($0 \leq \beta \leq 1$).

The product development manager's problem is to find a stationary admission policy that maximizes the total discounted reward over an infinite horizon. The state of our system at each decision point is represented by the number of available servers n combined with the payoff of the newest project idea, Π). Two decisions are possible: accept or reject (putting the idea into the waiting buffer). The value function is:

$$V(n, \Pi) = \max \begin{cases} \text{Accept: } \Pi + \int_0^\infty \int_0^\infty V(n-1, x)\lambda e^{-[\lambda+(N-n)\mu+\beta]t}dF(x)dt \\ \quad + \int_0^\infty V(n,0)(N-n)\mu e^{-[\lambda+(N-n)\mu+\beta]t}dt, \\ \text{Reject: } \int_0^\infty \int_0^\infty V(n,x)\lambda e^{-[\lambda+(N-n+1)\mu+\beta]t}dF(x)dt \\ \quad + \int_0^\infty V(n+1,\Pi)(N-n+1)\mu e^{-[\lambda+(N-n+1)\mu+\beta]t}dt. \end{cases}$$

$$(5.1)$$

Acceptance (first branch) implies an immediate reward Π, and then either a new idea arrives (first integral), or a capacity "slot" becomes available (second integral). Rejection has two possible outcomes: either

---

[3]This is common in NPD organizations: "We did not have enough capacity, but now we do!"
[4]This provides an approximate way of modelling idea obsolescence after some time.

a newer project idea arrives, or capacity frees up, enabling reconsidera-
tion of the current project idea (first and second integral, respectively).

When there is no idea pending for service, the value function depends
solely upon future arrivals and service completions, and no decision has
to be made:

$$V(n,0) = \int_0^\infty \left[(N-n)\mu \ V(n+1,0) + \int_0^\infty \lambda \ V(n,x)dF(x) \right] \ e^{-[\lambda+(N-n)\mu+\beta]t} \ dt.$$

$$(5.2)$$

Equations (5.1) and (5.2) can be simplified, based on the following
equality:

$$\int_0^\infty \int_0^\infty V(n,x)\lambda e^{-[\lambda+s\mu+\beta]t} dF(x)dt \ = \ \frac{\lambda}{\lambda+s\mu+\beta} \int_0^\infty V(n,x)dF(x)$$

$$\equiv \ \frac{\lambda}{\lambda+s\mu+\beta} \ J(n), \qquad (5.3)$$

and thus,

$$V(n,0) = \frac{\lambda \ J(n)}{\lambda+(N-n)\mu+\beta} + \frac{(N-n)\mu \ V(n+1,0)}{\lambda+(N-n)\mu+\beta}. \qquad (5.4)$$

The Bellman equation now becomes:

$$V(n,\Pi) = \max \begin{cases} \Pi + V(n-1,0), \\ V(n,0) + \frac{(N-n)\mu}{\lambda+(N-n)\mu+\beta}[V(n+1,\Pi) - V(n+1,0)]. \end{cases} \qquad (5.5)$$

Equation (5.5) offers an intuitive representation of the decision. Acceptance leads to the immediate reward and to a system state with one fewer
slots and no project idea pending. Rejection leads to a system state with
n capacity slots and no project pending. However, there is an additional
benefit from the "option" of later adopting the currently rejected idea,
if more capacity becomes available before a new idea arrives.

3.   Optimal policy

In this section, we derive the optimal admission policy. We first prove two useful lemmas.

LEMMA 5.1 *The optimal value function $V(n, \Pi)$ is convex non-decreasing in Π.*

Proof. All proofs are provided in the Appendix.

LEMMA 5.2 *The optimal value function $V(n, \Pi)$ is non-decreasing in n.*

Using the two lemmas, we now characterize the optimal admission policy.

THEOREM 5.1 *The optimal admission policy is a threshold policy. That is, in any state (n, Π), accept the current project if and only if $\Pi \geq \rho(n) \in \mathbf{R}_+$, the unique threshold value when n capacity slots are available.*

We now derive in closed form two characteristics of the value function (for $N = 2$): it has decreasing returns in n (Theorem 5.2), and the thresholds decrease in the number of open slots (Theorem 5.3). In other words, additional slots become less and less valuable, and the organization should become more choosy, the more capacity it has available.

THEOREM 5.2 *For $N = 2$, $\rho(i) \leq \rho(i - 1)$ for $i = 1, 2$, and $V(n, 0)$ exhibits decreasing returns.*

THEOREM 5.3 *For $N = 2$, the optimal value function is given by the solution to the following equations:*

$$(V_2 - V_1)[1 - F(V_2 - V_1)] - \int_{V_2-V_1}^{\infty} x dF(x) = -\frac{\beta}{\lambda} V_2 \tag{5.6}$$

$$(V_1 - V_0)[1 - F(V_1 - V_0)] - \int_{k_1}^{\infty} x dF(x) - \int_{V_2-V_1}^{k_1} (x - V_2 + V_1) dF(x) = \frac{\mu}{\lambda} V_2 - \frac{\mu + \beta}{\lambda} V_1 \tag{5.7}$$

$$\frac{2\mu + \beta}{2\mu}(\lambda + 2\mu + \beta) V_0 = (\lambda + 3\mu + 2\beta) V_1 - \mu V_2 \tag{5.8}$$

where $V_i = V(i, 0)$, and $k_1 = (\frac{1}{\lambda+\beta})(V_1 - V_0) + \frac{\mu}{\lambda+\mu+\beta}(V_2 - V_1)$,

and therefore

$$V(2, \Pi) = \begin{cases} \Pi + V(1, 0), & \Pi > V_2 - V_1 \\ V(2, 0) & otherwise. \end{cases} \tag{5.9}$$

$$V(1, \Pi) = \begin{cases} V(1, 0) + \frac{\mu}{\lambda+\mu+\beta}(\Pi - V_2 + V_1), & \Pi > V_2 - V_1 \\ V(1, 0). \end{cases} \tag{5.10}$$

and

$$V(0, \Pi) = \begin{cases} V(0, 0) + \frac{2\mu^2}{(\lambda+\mu+\beta)(\lambda+2\mu+\beta)}(\Pi - V_2 + V_1), & \Pi > V_2 - V_1 \\ V(0, 0). \end{cases} \tag{5.11}$$

4.   Discussion and Conclusion

The threshold policy derived in Theorem 5.1 has a direct managerial implication: management should not accept every arriving project idea, even if there is available capacity.[5] In other words, some attractive

---

[5]The exception is the very special case where the threshold is zero.

current ideas should be rejected not because they do not have a positive NPV, but because they would occupy valuable capacity that might be demanded by even more attractive future ideas. This is, of course, no different from known queueing results, extending them to a continuous value distribution of the "customers". Nevertheless, this lesson is still all-too-often neglected in NPD organizations, even when it has been learned for the manufacturing organization (e.g., Wheelwright and Clark 1992a; Reinertsen 1997).

The implications of Theorems 5.2 and 5.3 are intuitive: the value function is concave increasing in the number of open capacity slots (Theorem 5.2). The more open capacity slots the organization has, the less valuable is opening an additional one; an investment in NPD capacity has decreasing returns. Moreover, the organization should become *less selective* as more capacity slots are available. In Theorem 5.3 we characterize the thresholds and the optimal value function in closed form, under general conditions (e.g. for any distribution of project payoffs). The decreasing returns and decreasing thresholds are intuitive - a lot of free capacity implies accepting (almost) all valuable ideas, thus additional capacity is less useful.

However, the closed form characterization of thresholds and value functions, without restrictive assumptions, is often difficult to obtain.

The generality of our model is limited by two critical assumptions: first, our organization is "frictionless" – multiple projects running in parallel do not interfere with one another. This is not always true in reality – an organization that has many projects running in parallel requires multitasking of individual departments and personnel, which causes switch-overs and inefficiencies. We have seen multiple examples of companies hitting gridlock because of too much multitasking (see also Goldratt 1997). This clearly limits the increasing returns of NPD capacity in practice. However, the result may be a good approximation for the high-priority core efforts of the organization, for which enough capacity is made available.

The second critical assumption is that the value of a project idea is unrelated to its processing demands (we have assumed the two distributions to be independent). Again, this is not true in practice – clearly, large projects are typically required to yield higher returns. However, there is empirical evidence that project value is indeed weakly related to its resource requirements within limits – strategic fit and application focus can dominate resource expenditures (see Terwiesch and Loch 1999).

Finally, we have analyzed the decreasing returns of capacity only for the case of $N = 2$ (we are working on extending the result). It is important for NPD managers to identify circumstances under which investments in capacity have increasing returns, and much work remains to do so.

APPENDIX 5.A

Proof of Lemma 5.1. We proceed by induction. Take $n = N$ (all capacity is available). The value function (5.5) simplifies to:

$$V(N, \Pi) = \max \ \{\Pi + V(N - 1, 0), V(N, 0)\}. \qquad (5.A.1)$$

As both decision branches are non-decreasing in Π, $V(N, \Pi)$ is also non-decreasing in Π. In addition, $V(N, \Pi)$ is the maximum of two convex functions (specifically, $V(N, 0)$ does not depend on Π at all) and is, therefore, convex.

Now, assume that $V(k, \Pi)$ is convex non-decreasing in Π. The Bellman equation for $V(k - 1, \Pi)$ is:

$$V(k - 1, \Pi) = \max \left\{ \begin{array}{l} \Pi + V(k - 2, 0) \\ V(k - 1, 0) + \frac{(N-k+1)\mu}{\lambda + (N-k+1)\mu + \beta}[V(k, \Pi) - V(k, 0)]. \end{array} \right. \qquad (5.A.2)$$

Again, both decision branches are non-decreasing in Π. The acceptance branch is linear in Π, and the rejection branch is convex by the induction assumption. Thus, $V(k - 1, \Pi)$ is convex as the maximum of two convex functions. $\qquad \square$

Proof of Lemma 5.2.   Consider two otherwise identical systems that start in states (n, Π) and $(n + 1, \Pi)$, respectively. That is, while system 2 has an additional capacity slot available, both systems face the same (arbitrary) sample path of arrivals. Suppose we adopt the optimal admission policy in system 1, and we duplicate the action taken for each arrival in system 2. Note that the two systems differ in their rate of capacity slots opening up (the rate is $(N - k)\mu$ when k slots are available). Let $n_i(t)$ denote the number of open slots in system i at time t under the identical admission decisions (but possibly different sequences of capacity opening events).

We define two stopping times: Let T_1 be the first time when both systems have the same number of open slots (and, thus, the same system state, as both face the same arrivals): $T_1 = \min\{t : \ n_1(t) = n_2(t)\}$. Let T_2 be the first time at which system 1 reaches zero capacity availability: $T_2 = \min\{t : \ n_1(t) = 0\}$. We can now distinguish two cases: (1) $T_1 < T_2$ (system 1's available capacity catches up with system 2's available capacity before hitting zero), and (2) $T_1 > T_2$ (system 1's capacity hits zero before catching up with system 2).[6]

---

[6]We do not need to consider $T_1 = T_2$ because the probability that 2 events, an arrival and a slot opening in system 1, happen at the same time is zero.

In case (1), the rewards earned in both systems up to time T_1 are identical (by assumption). At time T_1, both systems enter an identical state. Thus, the optimal policy for system 1 from now on is also optimal for system 2, and the expected rewards from then on (the value function) are identical. Thus, in case (1), both systems have the same expected discounted payoff.[7]

In case (2), the state of system 1 at time T_2 is $(0,0)$ because it reaches zero capacity directly after an acceptance, so there is no idea pending at this point. As system 2 accepts the same idea, its state is $(k,0)$ for some $k > 0$ (remember that in case (2), system 2 has a larger number of open slots). We now have to consider two sub-cases: (2a) a slot opens in system 1 before a new idea arrives, and (2b), a new idea arrives before a new slot opens in system 1.

In case (2a), we keep going as before, replicating the decisions of system 1 in system 2 until either system 1 again hits zero capacity (go back to case 2) or until both systems' states become identical (we reach T_2, going to case 1).

In case (2b), system 1 must reject the idea, no matter what its payoff is (there is no capacity). System 2 can accept the idea, earning some positive reward. After accepting the idea, system 2 either reaches state $(0,0)$, and we go to case (1), or it still has $k - 1 > 0$, so it continues to replicate system 1's admission decisions until either case (1) or case (2) arises.

This argument shows that system 2 never does worse than system 1 until one of the stopping times is reached (or forever, if both are infinite), and then either does better (accepting an extra idea) or is stochastically identical to system 1. Furthermore, the value function $V(n+1, \Pi)$ is the result of the optimal policy, which is at least as good as the policy used by system 2 (replicating system 1). Thus, $V(n+1, \Pi) > V(n, \Pi)$.

□

Proof of Theorem 5.1. It suffices to show that the acceptance option of the optimal value function increases faster in Π than the rejection option. In combination with $V(n, \Pi)$ increasing in Π (Lemma 5.1), this implies that acceptance is the optimal choice whenever Π is above a threshold $\rho(n)$.

---

[7]Both systems also have the same payoff if both $T_1 = T_2 = \infty$.

We take the derivative of the value function (5.5) with respect to Π:

$$\frac{\partial V(n,\Pi)}{\partial \Pi} = \max \begin{cases} 1 & \text{(accept)}, \\ \frac{(N-n)\mu}{\lambda+(N-n)\mu+\beta} \frac{\partial V(n+1,\Pi)}{\partial \Pi} & \text{(reject)}. \end{cases} \tag{5.A.3}$$

Similarly, we can write for $(n+1)$ open slots:

$$\frac{\partial V(n+1,\Pi)}{\partial \Pi} = \{1 \quad \text{or} \quad \frac{(N-n-1)\mu}{\lambda+(N-n-1)\mu+\beta} \frac{\partial V(n+2,\Pi)}{\partial \Pi}\}. \tag{5.A.4}$$

Applying the same argument repeatedly, we obtain:

$$\frac{\partial V(n,\Pi)}{\partial \Pi} = \max \begin{cases} 1 & \text{accepted now} \\ \frac{(N-n)\mu}{\lambda+(N-n)\mu+\beta} & \text{accepted at } (n+1) \\ \frac{(N-n)\mu}{\lambda+(N-n)\mu+\beta}\frac{(N-n-1)\mu}{\lambda+(N-n-1)\mu+\beta} & \text{accepted at } (n+2) \\ \quad ... \\ \frac{(N-n)\mu}{\lambda+(N-n)\mu+\beta}\frac{(N-n-1)\mu}{\lambda+(N-n-1)\mu+\beta}\cdots\frac{\mu}{\lambda+\mu+\beta} & \text{accepted at } (N) \\ 0 & \text{if } n=0. \end{cases} \tag{5.A.5}$$

The last derivative is zero because there is no option to wait for an additional capacity server at the capacity limit. Thus, the derivative of the rejection option with respect to Π cannot be above 1, which implies that the value of the acceptance option increases faster in Π than the rejection option. This implies a unique threshold $\rho(n)$, above which all ideas are optimally accepted. It is the solution of:

$$\begin{aligned} \rho(n) &= [V(n,0) - V(n-1,0)] \\ &+ \frac{(N-n)\mu}{\lambda+(N-n)\mu+\beta}[V(n+1,\rho(n)) - V(n+1,0)]. \end{aligned} \tag{5.A.6}$$

Given that the value function is bounded above by $V(N,0) + \Pi$, $\rho(n)$ is a finite real number. □

Proof of Theorem 5.2.   We will prove it by contradiction. Assume $\rho_1 < \rho_2$. We can easily verify from (5.5) that the optimality equations for $n{=}1,2$ are

$$V(n,\Pi) = \max \begin{cases} \Pi + V(n-1,0), \\ V(n,0). \end{cases} \tag{5.A.7}$$

because of our assumption on the thresholds. An immediate consequence of the latter derivation is that $V_2 - V_1 > V_1 - V_0$, that is the optimal value function has increasing returns.

Hence, we can write the value expectation $J(n)$ by integrating over all possible values of Π. Keep also in mind that the equations (5.2) associate the $J(n)$ values to the V_n. Algebra leads us to the following two equations:

$$(V_2 - V_1)[1 - F(V_2 - V_1)] - \int_{V_2 - V_1}^{\infty} x dF(x) = -\frac{\beta}{\lambda} V_2 \qquad (5.A.8)$$

$$(V_1 - V_0)[1 - F(V_1 - V_0)] - \int_{V_1 - V_0}^{\infty} x dF(x) = \frac{\mu}{\lambda} V_2 - \frac{\mu + \beta}{\lambda} V_1 \qquad (5.A.9)$$

Now define the function

$$G(t) = t[1 - F(t)] - \int_t^{\infty} x dF(x) \qquad (5.A.10)$$

The first order derivative of $G(.)$ is $G'(t) = 1 - F(t)$, which for every cumulative probability distribution $F(.)$ is positive, hence $G(.)$ is increasing in its argument. Therefore, if $V_2 - V_1 > V_1 - V_0$ it should be $G(V_2 - V_1) > G(V_1 - V_0)$ and from our analysis above

$$-\tfrac{\beta}{\lambda} V_2 > \tfrac{\mu}{\lambda} V_2 - \tfrac{\mu + \beta}{\lambda} V_1$$

which leads to $V_2 > V_1$, an obvious contradiction according to Lemma 5.2. Therefore, our assumption can not hold and $\rho_1 \geq \rho_2$ $\qquad\qquad\square$

Proof of Theorem 5.3. We know that $\rho_1 \geq \rho_2$ which implies that the Bellman equation for $n = 1$ becomes:

$$V(1, \Pi) = \max \begin{cases} \Pi + V_0, \\ V_1 + \frac{\mu}{\lambda + \mu + \beta}[V(2, \Pi) - V_2]. \end{cases} \qquad (5.A.11)$$

Integration over all possible values for Π, provides in closed form the $J(1)$ value, and with the use of (5.2) equations we get the following equation:

$$(V_1 - V_0)[1 - F(V_1 - V_0)] - \int_{V_1 - V_0}^{\infty} x dF(x) - \frac{\mu}{\lambda + \mu + \beta} \int_{V_2 - V_1}^{k_1} (x - V_2 + V_1) dF(x) = \frac{\mu}{\lambda} V_2 - \frac{\mu + \beta}{\lambda} V_1 \qquad (5.A.12)$$

where, $k_1 = (\frac{1}{\lambda + \beta})(V_1 - V_0) + \frac{\mu}{\lambda + \mu + \beta}(V_2 - V_1)$ is the value of the threshold for capacity $n = 1$.

The equivalent equation for $V(2, \Pi)$ stays the same as the one calculated in the proof of Theorem 5.2 (5.6).

In order to obtain the third equation it is sufficient to look at the Bellman equation for $n = 0$. Then we have:

$$V(0, \Pi) = \frac{\lambda}{\lambda + 2\mu + \beta} J(0) + \frac{2\mu}{\lambda + 2\mu + \beta} V(1, \Pi) \qquad (5.A.13)$$

Integration leads to

$$J(0) = \frac{2\mu}{2\mu + \beta} J(1) \qquad (5.A.14)$$

hence, substituting the $J(1), J(0)$ from the (5.2) equations, we get

$$\frac{2\mu + \beta}{2\mu}(\lambda + 2\mu + \beta)V_0 = (\lambda + 3\mu + 2\beta)V_1 - \mu V_2 \qquad (5.A.15)$$

The triad of the above equations provides solutions for the V_i's which are the basis for the closed form expressions of the $V(i, \Pi)$. In order now to obtain the closed form expressions we substitute the V_i's and the calculated thresholds in the Bellman optimality equations.

Hence, for example, in the $V(1, \Pi)$ it is sufficient to observe that $V(0, 0) + \Pi$ at $\Pi = \rho(1)$ is equal to the $V(1, 0) + \frac{\mu}{\lambda + \mu + \beta}(\Pi - V_2 + V_1)$

which proves the constant slope linear portion of the optimal value function.

□

Chapter 6

PRIORITIZING ONGOING PROJECTS DURING EXECUTION

1. Introduction

New product development (NPD) organizations pursue many projects in parallel, in order to achieve broader product lines (mass customization) and higher market share (e.g., Reinertsen 1997; Ulrich and Eppinger 2003; Cusumano and Nobeoka 1998). In multi-project environments, it happens commonly that projects compete for access to a scarce resource.[1] The processing time that each project spends at the resource is much shorter than the projects' total duration. Examples of such scarce resources are equipment (such as an acoustic analyzer or wind channel in automotive design) or uniquely specialized areas of expertise, such as a critical department (e.g., a testing lab), or individuals (e.g., an engineer mastering a highly specialized procedure). Such scarce resources, although representing only a small part of the project's total duration,

---

[1]This chapter is based on Kavadias S., and C. H. Loch 2003. "Dynamic Prioritization of Projects at a Scarce Resource." *Production and Operations Management* 12(4).

can become bottlenecks, and resource allocation is a critical factor for profitability (Adler *et al.* 1995).

How should a scarce resource be allocated among ongoing projects, or, how should projects be awarded priority for the short execution time there, in order to maximize the portfolio value? Conflicts among project managers over access to the resource are common in project organizations. Rather than solving such conflicts via giving priority to the project manager "who screams the loudest", senior managers need robust prioritization criteria. Some previous literature has recommended working on the project with the highest ratio of value over processing time, without interruption, until it has finished the work at the scarce resource (e.g., Goldratt 1997, 125-130; Banerjee and Hopp 2001). This rule of thumb follows the $c\mu$ rule of scheduling (e.g., Van Mieghem 1995): work first on the project that suffers the highest delay cost per processing time unit. However, while this policy is dynamic, it does not allow recourse (reassessing an assignment while the job is being processed). This is not sufficient for NPD projects because their progress may be stochastic and may have to be re-examined mid course.

If projects are independent of one another and exponentially affected by delays (e.g., discounting), the dynamic problem is a multi-armed bandit (MAB). The optimal policy introduced by Gittins and Jones 1972 and Whittle 1980 assigns (at each decision point) the critical resource to the project with the highest index, i.e., each index represents the amount of money that would make "stopping" or "continuation" of the project equally attractive. This remains true if there is a common constant fixed changeover cost among projects (Banks and Sundaram 1994).

However, when projects are penalized non-exponentially for delays, independence, and thus decomposability, break down: the additional delay loss of one project depends on what happens to other projects (e.g., how much time the predecessor requires). Therefore, the problem becomes a "restless bandit". It is NP-hard and has not been solved in general because projects are interdependent. In this chapter, we show that an intuitive and easily implementable policy is optimal if three assumptions hold. First, the delay cost is an increasing fraction of the payoff, independent of the performance state. Second, costs are not discounted. Third, projects are not abandoned, based on their performance state during their processing at the scarce resource.

These assumptions are realistic in an NPD context because processing at any individual scarce resource is very short (e.g., a few days) compared to the total project duration (months or years). Thus, discounting during processing at the scarce resource can be ignored. Still, even a few days' delay may make the difference between defeating competition or not, and thus heavily impact revenues (Clark 1989). Third, while projects may be modified to counteract negative results obtained at the scarce resource (e.g., a test), they are rarely abandoned at this point (see, e.g., Balachandra 1984).

In the optimal policy, the scarce resource is allocated to the project with the highest total delay loss *as if* it were delayed until one of the other projects is completed. Thus, the prioritization "pretends" that each project is delayed all the way until the currently worked upon project is completed, although the dynamic policy re-evaluates the prioritization in between. This is similar to the $c\mu$ rule in dynamic scheduling, while additionally including non-linear delay costs and recourse after processing has begun.

We describe the decision model and derive the optimal index policy in Section 2 of this chapter. Section 3 discusses examples and managerial implications.

2.   Model and Optimal Sequencing Policy

Suppose K projects are waiting for access to a specialized resource. At any point in time, the resource can work only on one project. Time t_k is discrete and denotes the number of stages *remaining* for project k to complete its work at the scarce resource if it has continuous access to it. A stage corresponds to a phase of processing (e.g., setup, identification of technical sensitivities, data collection, evaluation). Stage k takes $\tau_k(t_k)$ time periods (say, days). At the end of each stage, a measure of currently assessed performance $x_k \epsilon \mathcal{X}_k(t_k)$ (the performance state) is reviewed, which we assume to be one-dimensional (such as the clock speed of a computer CPU).[2] Note that in our context, the total processing time

---

[2]Performance is measured directly, e.g., as speed, cost, or features, or if the product has multiple attributes, as a composite metric of the attribute bundle as in conjoint analysis.

at the scarce resource (typically, days or weeks) is much shorter than the completion time for the entire project (typically, months or years).

Transition among performance states is Markovian with known probabilities $p_{x_k y_k}$. For example, the project may go according to plan (no change in performance state), or better or worse than planned. Each project incurs a cost $c_k(x_k, t_k)$ per time unit, paid at the transition from stage t_k to $t_k - 1$ (e.g., the daily cost rate of work accumulates over the stage, and it depends on the nature of work during that stage).

The performance state at $t_k = 0$, when a project has finished its work at the scarce resource, determines its payoff $\Pi_k(x_k)$. This payoff determines the expectation of the discounted final reward when the project is completed, and it is typically non-decreasing in the performance state. If delays are uniformly costly (discounting), the payoff depends only on the project's performance state, which makes the problem an MAB.

In general, NPD projects differ in their delay costs. Delay costs matter greatly in NPD, as time-to-market is often extremely important. The opportunity cost of time is often greater than the budget benefits of cost savings, as a delay may put a product behind the competition, reducing market share and lifetime revenues (Blackburn 1991; Goldratt 1997; Ittner and Larcker 1997). For example, PCs have product life cycles of 6-8 months. A one-month introduction delay severely reduces lifecycle profitability of a model (e.g., Loch 1999), whereas Clark 1989 notes that "each day of delay for the introduction of an average automobile has been estimated to cost \$1 million" (Clark 1989, 1260). Timely

project execution can result in visible impact on share value (Hendricks

and Singhal 1997; Datar *et al.* 1997). Therefore, even a delay during

the short processing at the scarce resource may significantly impact the

project's ultimate payoff at its completion.

We expand the state space to track the total amount of delay that a

project has experienced since its start, denoted as d_k. We assume that

a delay reduces a project's payoff multiplicatively, in the form of

$$\widetilde{\Pi}_k(x_k, d_k) = \Pi_k(x_k) \cdot f_k(d_k). \tag{6.1}$$

Thus, $\Pi_k(x_k)$ is the project's "potential" payoff if delivered on sched-

ule, and the *delay loss function* $f_k(d_k)$ decreases in the total delay d_k,

reducing the potential payoff. A delay loss may be caused by missing

a market window, or by a clause in the project contract specifying a

penalty that increases with the delay. As we discussed above, we can

realistically assume that the discount rate $\delta = 0$ during the short time

spent at the scarce resource, and prioritization reviews at the scarce

resource are even shorter.

Denote the individual value function of project k as $V_k(x_k, t_k, d_k)$. We

do not consider the option of completely abandoning projects. This as-

sumption is analogous to the assumption in dynamic scheduling models,

and captures the context which motivates this study – projects are not

canceled while at a specialized resource, only re-prioritized. Termina-

tion decisions happen at progress reviews or after special events. Project abandonment would be relevant if the critical resource was shared through-out the project. In this setup, we can write the value function of an individual project.

PROPOSITION 6.1 *The value function of project k in isolation is*

$$V_k(x_k, t_k, d_k) = -EC_k(x_k, t_k) + E[\Pi_k \mid x_k, t_k] \, f_k(d_k), \tag{6.2}$$

$$E[\Pi_k \mid x_k, t_k] = \sum_{s_1} \cdots \sum_{s_i} \{p_{x_k s_1} p_{s_1 s_2} \cdots p_{s_{t_k-1} s_{t_k}} \Pi_k(s_{t_k})\} \tag{6.3}$$

is the expected potential final payoff, and

$$EC_k(x_k, t_k) = c_k(x_k, t_k)\tau_k(t_k) + \sum_{s_1} p_{x_k s_1} c(s_1, t_k - 1)\tau_k(t_k - 1)(\ldots$$

$$(\sum_{s_2} p_{s_1 s_2} c(s_2, t_k - 2)\tau_k(t_k - 2)(\sum_{s_{t_k-1}} p_{s_{t_k-2} s_{t_k-1}} c(s_{t_k-1}, 1)\tau_k(1)))\ldots) \tag{6.4}$$

is the expected remaining execution cost at the scarce resource.

Thus, we have formulated each project's value function as the *potential payoff* expectation reduced by the delay loss accumulated *up to now*, minus the expected remaining project costs. Based on this representation, we first characterize the optimal policy for two projects. Call $T_k = \sum_{l=1}^{t_k} \tau_k(l)$ the remaining processing time of project k.

THEOREM 6.1 *With two projects, it is optimal to work on the project with the larger "expected delay loss", calculated as if it were started only after uninterrupted completion of the other project at the scarce resource:*

$$(f_i(d_i) - f_i(d_i + T_j))E[\Pi_i \mid x_i, t_i].$$

The expected delay loss criterion "pretends" that the project will be de-layed until the other project finishes, although the dynamic policy allows recourse at the following decision point. If the states did not change in the future, it would indeed be optimal to perform the projects sequen-tially, without interruption (van Oyen *et al.* 1992 call this "exhaustive policies"). But this does not mean that either project actually *will* be completed without interruption. As the optimal policy depends on the project states, the decision next period may switch if the project that was worked upon has deteriorated.

The decision rule in Theorem 6.1 is a discrete version of the $c\mu$ rule with different delay costs across projects and with recourse while a project, or job, is being processed. The project that loses the most (corresponding to c_i) while the other project has access to the critical resource (corresponding to μ_i or $\frac{1}{T_i}$) receives highest priority. In one spe-cial case, our optimal policy collapses to a "shortest expected processing time" rule.

Corollary. *If the two projects have the same expected potential payoff and the same delay loss function, it is optimal to allocate the critical resource to the project with the **shortest remaining completion time**.*

☐

The general policy, as stated in Theorem 6.1, only holds for two projects. When $K > 2$, *all combinations* of project orderings must be compared in order to find the optimal policy. The number of orderings increases geometrically with K (although dominated cases can be excluded where a project is interrupted by another project that finishes later). Theorem 6.2 shows that the maximum delay loss policy does apply also for $K > 2$, but the index may not find an optimal ordering when the delay cost comparison is "circular". Finding the optimal ordering is guaranteed only when delay losses are *linear*:

$$f_i(d_i) = 1 - a_i d_i. \tag{6.5}$$

Here, a_i represents the payoff loss *per period* of project i being delayed. The linear case is a good approximation in a number of important situations in practice, when delay losses may be non-linear over a span of months or years, but are close to linear over the days or weeks during which projects compete for a given scarce resource.

THEOREM 6.2 *Suppose K projects share a critical resource. Then it is optimal to allocate the resource to project i with the highest expected delay loss in each review period such that for all $j \neq i$, and $\tau \in (0, \sum_i T_i)$:*

$$[f_i(t_i + d_i + \tau) - f_i(t_i + d_i + T_j + \tau)]E[\Pi_i \mid x_i, t_i]$$
$$\geq [f_j(t_j + d_j + \tau) - f_j(t_j + d_j + T_i + \tau)]E[\Pi_j \mid x_j, t_j]. \tag{6.6}$$

If delay losses are non-linear, it may not be possible to find an optimal sequence fulfilling (6.6). If, however, delay losses are linear as in (6.5), (6.6) can be simplified to $\tau = 0$ and, moreover, there is always a project that satisfies (6.6). □

The problem that there may be no project fulfilling (6.6) is serious. The reason is that (6.6) must hold for all values of τ, that is, the prioritized project must have the highest delay loss, no matter whether coming second, third, or last. This is so restrictive that the index will often be circular and not find the optimal sequence. Consider the following simple example: There are three one-stage and one-period projects with deterministic payoffs $\mathbf{V} = (100, 100, 190)$. Their delay functions (for one and two periods of delay) are $f_1 = (0.7; 0.665)$, $f_2 = (0.85; 0.6375)$, and $f_3 = (0.9; 0.81)$. Then the projects' losses over delays of one and two periods are described in Figure 6.1:

Project	Delay loss (1st period)	Delay loss (2nd period)
1	30	33.50
2	15	36.25
3	19	36.10

Figure 6.1. Data of Example With Circular Sequencing Index

There is no best ordering based on the delay losses. Thus, the index does not find the optimal sequencing (which is 3-2-1, with a total value of 341.5).

However, the index *does* find the optimal sequence if the delay losses are linear. As we mentioned above, this is a good approximation when the processing time at the scarce resource is short compared to the entire project. In this case, not only does the index always find an ordering, but moreover, we only need to compare pairs of projects one-on-one, as if either came first. This is because the delay loss from letting the other project go first is always the same, no matter whether another project comes before both or not. Thus, the policy becomes very easy to implement.

The optimality conditions (6.6) can again be interpreted as a version of the $c\mu$ rule, as we discussed under Theorem 6.1. The direct linkage to the $c\mu$ rule becomes apparent in the linear delay losses case. When delay losses obey (6.5), (6.6) can be written as follows:

$$a_i t_j E[\Pi_i \mid x_i, t_i] > a_j t_i E[\Pi_j \mid x_j, t_j] \text{ or}$$

$$\frac{a_i}{t_i} E[\Pi_i \mid x_i, t_i] > \frac{a_j}{t_j} E[\Pi_j \mid x_j, t_j].$$

Defining $\frac{1}{T_i}$ as the "processing rate" μ_i of project i, and $a_i E_{t_i}[\Pi_i \mid x_i, t_i]$ as the marginal delay cost for project i, we see that what is compared across the two projects is a $c\mu$ quantity. Thus, the optimal policy *is* the $c\mu$ rule extended for intermediate reviews.

3. Discussion and Examples

3.1 Importance of Recourse

While it is optimal to start working on the project with the greatest expected delay loss as if the other project was finished first all the way, this priority should be revisited. The optimality of recourse is not unan-

imously accepted (Goldratt 1997; Banerjee and Hopp 2001). Goldratt
is particularly vocal, and dismisses repeated switching with the argument: "multitasking is the killer of lead times." We present a simple
illustrative example to inspire the reader's intuition as to why recourse
is important.

Consider the two projects in Figure 6.2. They compete for access to a
testing lab. Both require two processing stages, the outcomes of which
determine the expected project payoff. From experience, the expected
final payoffs (shown in boxes) and outcome probabilities (shown on the
arrows) are known. Project 1 has an expected value of 111 and project
2 of 109. Project 1 has a concave delay loss function $f_1(d)$: $f_1(1) = 0.85$
and $f_1(2) = 0.595$. The loss function of project 2 is convex: $f_2(1) = 0.7$
and $f_2(2) = 0.56$.

First, it is not necessarily optimal to prioritize the project with the
higher expected payoff: Project 2 would suffer an expected delay loss of
47.8 if project 1 was done first, versus 44.4 the other way round. Thus,
project 2 should start, resulting in an expected portfolio payoff of 174.7
(versus 171.8 if project 1 starts). This is, of course, not new.

What *is* new is that it is optimal to switch after the first stage if
project 2 has a negative test outcome. In this case, its expected value
has shrunk to 13, and its delay loss (from two periods' delay) to 5.7.
Project 1, in contrast, would suffer an additional delay loss, from the

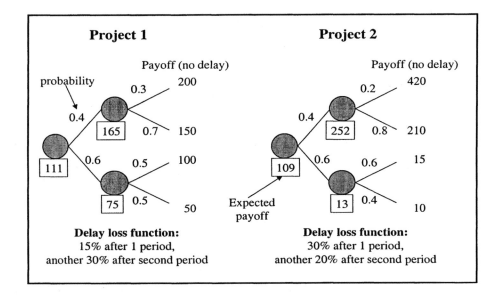

Figure 6.2. Two Projects Competing for a Scarce Resource

second period, of 28.3. Thus, it is optimal to allow switching, which increases the optimal portfolio value to 188.2.

3.2 Limitations Under Stochastic Delay Losses

The "expected delay loss index" with recourse holds under three realistic assumptions in the context of projects competing for access at a specialist resource: the delay loss does not depend on the project performance, costs are not discounted, and projects are not canceled while at the scarce resource.

There is an additional important limitation, namely that project progress through the stages (at the scarce resource) must be deterministic. This is sometimes true (e.g., when a fixed set of tests or procedures must be performed), but may also not be the case (e.g., when certain tests must be repeated, depending on their outcome). A simple example shows why *schedule uncertainty* invalidates optimality of the index.

Suppose we have two projects, each lasting one period (say, one week), with probability p_i, or having to go through a correction loop lasting another week with probability $(1 - p_i)$. Project 1 has a convex delay loss: a delay by only one week reduces its payoff a lot, while the second week of delay makes almost no difference (for example, because there is a deadline in one week). Project 2, in contrast, has a concave delay loss: a delay by one week is not very detrimental, while the second week of delay does a lot of damage (e.g., there is a deadline in 2 weeks). In this case, it may be optimal to start with project 1 for one week. If it does finish, everything is fine, and project 2 can finish with one week of delay (and little delay loss). If project 1 is delayed after one week, one switches to project 2, to prevent it from suffering a large loss – project 1 is already suffering its largest loss anyway. If projects are cancelled or abandoned during processing at the scarce resource, it can be shown in a similar way that the priority index is not optimal.[3]

These two examples show that schedule delays and project abandonment destroy the separability of the project value functions in the presence of delay loss functions other than pure financial discounting. All easily implementable index policies may fundamentally fail and lead to wrong conclusions.

---

[3]In an MAB model such as Banerjee and Hopp 2001, project abandonment leaves the index intact because all projects are discounted exponentially and suffer no additional delay losses.

4. Conclusion

While we have focused on the selection of projects in Chapters 3-5, this chapter focuses on allocating a scarce resource among a set of ongoing projects that are time-critical. We characterize the optimal dynamic resource allocation policy in an important case that is typical for NPD situations: delay losses are a revenue fraction that increases with the length of the delay, while being independent of the project performance.

The optimal policy extends the $c\mu$ rule from dynamic scheduling to project prioritization in NPD. Highest priority goes to the project that would suffer the highest payoff loss (corresponding to c) calculated as if the other project was completed uninterruptedly at the scarce resource (corresponding to μ). Our extension has two aspects: First, our optimality conditions hold for general non-linear cost structures, which previous work has shown only asymptotically under heavy traffic (G-$c\mu$, Van Mieghem 1995). The price we pay is that our policy is guaranteed to find an ordering only if the delay losses are approximated by linear functions. Second, while previous work has allowed switching among projects only when the server naturally frees up, our dynamic policy awards priority *as if* projects were not interrupted in the future, but *does* allow switching (recourse) during service. Recourse has not been unanimously accepted in previous work (Goldratt 1997; Banerjee and Hopp 2001).

Our results have important managerial implications for the difficult challenge of dynamic project prioritization during execution, which often causes friction and confusion. Although general "strategic" priorities are sometimes established, these priorities are too coarse to resolve conflicts over a piece of equipment, a week's work capacity of a specialist, or access to a testing lab. As projects' fortunes and urgency levels change over their duration, additional guidelines are needed about how to resolve such conflicts. The normative results from the model in this chapter can be used as guidelines of this nature: if projects are urgent and in danger of being late to the market, priority is driven by the penalty of missing the market window. Changes in performance states and task durations may reverse the priorities dynamically.

Our model also verifies the limited applicability range of easily implementable index-like policies in a restless bandit (building on Gittins 1989): if general non-linear delay losses combine with project abandonment or stochastic delays, simple index-like rules are unreliable; one must experiment with more complex *ad hoc* rules that are adapted to the situation. Robust decision guidelines for allocating the NPD resource pool to a project portfolio are still sadly lacking.

APPENDIX 6.A

Proof of Proposition 6.1.   Equations (6.3) and (6.4) follow directly from the Markovian nature of the state transitions.   □

Proof of Theorem 6.1 We refer to the projects as i and j. Suppose i finishes first, but j is processed for Δ_j periods in between, interrupting i. Thus, j is delayed by the full duration T_i of project i, and thus the expected portfolio value is:

$$V_i = -\sum_{k=1}^{2} EC_k(x_k, t_k) + E[\Pi_i \mid x_i, t_i] \, f_i(d_i + \Delta_j) + E[\Pi_j \mid x_j, t_j] \, f_j(d_j + T_i).$$

In the same way, we can write the expected portfolio value resulting from finishing project i all the way first, without being interrupted:

$$V_i' = -\sum_{k=1}^{2} EC_k(x_k, t_k) + E[\Pi_i \mid x_i, t_i] \, f_i(d_i) + E[\Pi_j \mid x_j, t_j] \, f_j(d_j + T_i).$$

It is immediately clear that $V_i < V_i'$ because project i is finished earlier without delaying project j further (by exchanging the order of the ending stages of project i with the interrupting stages of project j). Analogously, we can argue that if project j finishes first, it is better to conduct it without interruption by project i. Thus, we have established that the portfolio value function is given by (where bold letters denote vectors):

$$V(\mathbf{x}, \mathbf{t}, \mathbf{d}) = -\sum_{k=1}^{2} EC_k(x_k, t_k) + \max \begin{cases} E[\Pi_i \mid x_i, t_i] \, f_i(d_i) + E[\Pi_j \mid x_j, t_j] \, f_j(d_j + T_i) \\ E[\Pi_j \mid x_j, t_j] \, f_j(d_j) + E[\Pi_i \mid x_i, t_i] \, f_i(d_i + T_j) \end{cases}$$

This is the value function "as if" either project was completed all the way without interruption by the other project. $\qquad\square$

Proof of Theorem 6.2 First we prove that if a project i fulfills (6.6), it should be worked on first, then that a project i fulfilling (6.6) can be found if (6.5) holds, but not necessarily otherwise.

The portfolio value function for K projects is $V^K(\mathbf{x}, \mathbf{t}, \mathbf{d}) = \max_k \{-c_k(x_k, t_k)\tau_k(t_k) + V(\mathbf{x}', \mathbf{t}', \mathbf{d} + \tau_k)\}$, where $\mathbf{x}'$ is the vector $\mathbf{x}$ with the kth element changed to y_k, $\mathbf{t}'$ is the vector $\mathbf{t}$ with the kth element reduced by one unit, and $\tau_k = (\tau_1, ..., \tau_{k-1}, 0, \tau_{k+1}, ...\tau_K)^T$.

The decomposability exhibited in Theorem 6.1 can be generalized to this case, following the same logic. The project that finishes first should be completed without interruption, being better off without further delaying the others. Then, the project finishing second should be completed without interruption, etc.

Let the set of all possible sequences of projects be S (it has $K!$ elements) with typical element s. Each s implies a project ordering, in which $[j]$ denotes the position (rank) of project j, and $rank[l]$ identifies the project holding position l in the ordering.

Then we can re-write the portfolio value function as:

$$V(\mathbf{x}, \mathbf{t}, \mathbf{d}) = \max_{s \in S} \{ \sum_{j=1}^{K} V_j(x_j, t_j, d_j + \sum_{l=1}^{[j]-1} T_{rank[l]}) \}. \qquad (6.A.1)$$

Now, we show that project i fulfilling (6.6) should be processed first. We can divide S into clusters: all s in cluster C_1 have i in first position, all s in cluster C_2 have project i in second position, and so on until cluster K, where i is last. From clusters 1 and 2, we can identify pairs for which the first and second projects are exchanged while all other positions remain the same:

$$V_i(x_i, t_i, d_i) + V_k(x_k, t_k, d_k + T_i) + \sum_{\substack{j \neq i,k \\ s \in C_1}} V_j(x_j, t_j, d_j + T_i + T_k + \sum_{l=3}^{[j]-1} T_{rank[l]}) \qquad (A)$$

$$V_k(x_k, t_k, d_k) + V_i(x_i, t_i, d_i + T_k) + \sum_{\substack{j \neq i,k \\ s \in C_2}} V_j(x_j, t_j, d_j + T_i + T_k + \sum_{l=3}^{[j]-1} T_{rank[l]}) \qquad (B).$$

By assumption that i fulfills (6.6) we have $E[\Pi_i \mid x_i, t_i](f_i(d_i) - f_i(d_i + T_k)) \geq E_{t_k}[\Pi_k \mid x_k, t_k](f_k(d_k) - f_k(d_k + T_i))$, which implies (A) > (B).

Analogously, we pair orderings from clusters 2 and 3, exchanging project positionings 2 and 3, and so on. Take an ordering of the other $(K-1)$ projects and call it s_{-i}. Denote with $(s_{-i}, [i] = n)$ the ordering resulting from inserting project i in nth position into s_{-i}. As a result of the above reasoning, we get for any s_{-i}: $V(s_{-i}, [i] = n) \geq V(s_{-i}, [i] = n+1)$ $\forall n < K$. This proves the first claim of the theorem.

While the first part of the proof does not use (6.5), linearity is required to guarantee the existence of a "best" project to be executed first. Assume (6.5) and call (one of) the ordering(s) maximizing the portfolio value function s^*. Call the project with rank 1 in s^* project i. Construct the same clusters as above with respect to this project i (s^* is thus in cluster 1). Take the sequence from cluster 2 that is associated with s^* (that is, the ordering is the same except that i is inserted in second instead of in first position). Exchange the first and second positions, and compare the resulting value functions. By assumption, the value function associated with s^* must be at least as high as any other:

$$V_i(x_i, t_i, d_i) + V_k(x_k, t_k, d_k + T_i) + \sum_{\substack{j \neq i,k \\ s \in C_1}} V_j(x_j, t_j, d_j + T_i + T_k + \sum_{l=3}^{[j]-1} T_{rank[l]})$$

$$\geq V_k(x_k, t_k, d_k) + V_i(x_i, t_i, d_i + T_k) + \sum_{\substack{j \neq i,k \\ s \in C_2}} V_j(x_j, t_j, d_j + T_i + T_k + \sum_{l=3}^{[j]-1} T_{rank[l]})$$

$$\Rightarrow \quad a_i t_k E[\Pi_i \mid x_i, t_i] \geq a_k t_i E_{t_k}[\Pi_k \mid x_k, t_k]. \tag{6.A.2}$$

We can perform the same comparison by exchanging the first and nth position between s^* and the associated sequence from cluster n, obtaining an analogous expression to (6.A.2). Together, these comparisons establish (6.6).

Finally, we show that a best project cannot always be found for non-linear delay loss functions. The reason is that the expected delay loss comparison may be "circular", as the following (easy to construct) example shows. Suppose that $E[\Pi_k \mid x_k, t_k] =$ \$937,375; \$506,069; and \$687,386 for the three projects, respectively. The delay loss rates are $(d_1, d_2, d_3) = (9, 16, 2)$ and the remaining project times are $(t_1, t_2, t_3) = (44, 16, 43)$ (taking $\tau_k(t_k) = 1$ for all k, t_k). Finally, the loss function is common to all three projects, $f_i(d) = 1 - \sqrt{0.001d}$.

The expected delay loss criterion comes out as follows: the delay loss of project 1 versus 2 (if 2 is completed first) is \$59,285, the loss of 2 versus 1 is \$59,948. Thus, project 2 has higher priority than 1. Similarly, the loss for 2 versus is 3 is \$58,911, while 3 versus 2 loses \$61,481. Project 3 is preferred. Finally, the loss of 1 versus 3 is \$124,827 compared to \$116,687 the other way around. Consequently, project 1 is preferred. This produces a circular rank order, so the expected delay loss criterion does not produce an implementable policy. □

Chapter 7

LESSONS FROM THIS STUDY: WHAT HAVE WE LEARNED?

What are the lessons for managers that emerge from this quite technical set of studies? In this final chapter, we draw some high-level conclusions that we believe to be relevant for managers responsible for portfolio management.

In order to look at portfolio management as a whole, it is useful to look at a representation of the development funnel (a term that was introduced by Wheelwright and Clark 1992a) as shown in Figure 7.1. The Figure identifies four major conceptual parts to portfolio management.

At the highest level, the context of making funding decisions is unstructured and messy; it depends on an uncertain future, actions by competitors, and a complexity of the overall "business problem" that defies orderly problem solving. This is the realm of strategy. While strategy is beyond the scope of this book, this certainly does not mean that strategy is not important. On the contrary, strategy provides a structured business proposition within which the organization can perform targeted problem solving. Strategy should align the actions of the various players, and provide "categories" of different types of NPD and R&D activities, each of which is homogenous enough to be managed

consistently. It is within these categories (for example, "next generation core product projects", or "2nd line technical support") where we
can hope to perform quantitative project selection in the sense of this
book. Good overviews of strategy can be found in Hamel and Prahalad
1989; Markides 1999; Hamel 2000; Roussel *et al.* 1991; Wheelwright and
Clark 1992a, and an example of strategic alignment of R&D in Loch
and Tapper 2002 and Kaplan and Norton 2000.

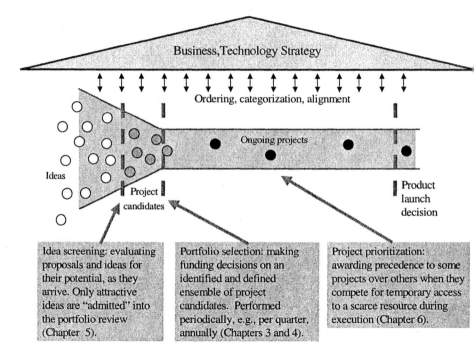

Figure 7.1. Portfolio Management in the Development Funnel

We add, here, one remark about the role of strategy: too often, organizations approach it too much as a "plan", which may be seen as a
competitive weapon in itself, and therefore perhaps be kept secret, even
from own employees. This approach not only overestimates the power
of strategy (indeed, the strategy field has moved away from planning
toward flexibility, see Williamson 1999; Hamel 2000), but it also fore-

goes the powerful function of strategy in providing a clear common goal around which an organization can coordinate.

Under the roof of strategy in Figure 7.1, there are then three conceptually distinct activities within portfolio management (that is, projects must be managed as an *ensemble*, not individually): idea screening, portfolio selection for funding, and ongoing prioritization. It is the second activity that has traditionally been emphasized in portfolio management literature in Operations Management. We address this activity in Chapters 3 and 4, observing that the problem is still messy enough (especially because of uncertain and fuzzy data availability) that simple methods, based a project ranking of the marginal benefit (project value per dollar of investment), may be more appropriate and usable than sophisticated combinatorial optimization methods.

We then widen the usual sense of "portfolio management" to also include idea screening and ongoing prioritization activities; both are so important that a good portfolio comes to nothing if they are not performed. Idea screening is related to an Operations Management sub-literature on "admission policies". Ideas must be evaluated as to whether they are promising enough to be considered further (e.g., to be analyzed for the subsequent funding decision). Chapter 5 develops a simple conceptual model of idea screening based on a "value potential" estimation. Again, we acknowledge the complexity of the problem by proposing a simple rule that is usable by managers: there is a value threshold below which projects are rejected.[1] The model formally supports the intuition that the organization should become less demanding as it has more NPD capacity available – NPD capacity has decreasing returns. Our closed

---

[1] In this simple model, all projects are assumed to require the same NPD capacity. In reality, the value threshold must be adjusted by the capacity use.

form solution may, with further work, be used to derive quantitative acceptance thresholds for real cases.

Finally, we include ongoing prioritization in the scope of portfolio management. Most NPD organizations have at least some scarce specialist resources that are shared across multiple projects (e.g., testing or analysis labs, access to a special site or equipment, etc.), and the portfolio funding decision simply does not settle who gets precedence at these scarce resources. This leads to considerable friction and tension in organizations that we have worked with. Again, we propose a simple rule that managers can apply – give priority to the project that suffers the largest delay loss if the other project goes first. However, we also establish the limit of such simple rules – for example, if processing times at the scarce resource are seriously unpredictable, the rule may not be optimal (and *ad hoc* criteria may have to be used).

In conclusion, the mathematical and technical effort in this book serves to accomplish two things: (a) characterize the *structure* of the optimization problem that the organization faces, and (b) to identify simple and implementable decision rules, for which we know under which circumstances they are optimal or near-optimal, and which are transparent and intuitive for practicing managers.

One may need to be a modeling specialist to identify the structure and to derive the decision rules, but understanding the structure and implementing the rules should *not* require modeling expertise. Classic mathematical programming methods have overlooked the second part of this statement, and introduced mathematical complexity, which we believe is the reason why they have not been widely adopted in practice.

References

Adler, P. S., Mandelbaum A., Nguyen V., and Schwerer E. 1995. "From Project to Process Management: An Empirically-Developed Framework for Analyzing Product Development Time". *Management Science* 41 (3), 458-484.

Aksin, O. Z., P. T. Harker. 2001. Modeling a Phone Center: Analysis of a Multichannel, Multiresource Processor Loss System. *Management Science* 47 (2), 324-336.

Ali A., Kalwani M. U., and Kovenock D. 1993. "Selecting Product Development Projects: Pioneering versus Incremental Innovation Strategies". *Management Science* 39 (3), 255-274.

Arthur W. B. 1994. *Increasing Returns and Path Dependence in the Economy.* University of Michigan Press, Ann Arbor.

Asawa M. and Teneketzis D. 1996. "Multi-Armed Bandits with Switching Penalties". *IEEE Transactions on Automatic Control* 41 (3), 328-348.

Balachandra R. 1984. "Critical Signals for Making Go/No Go Decisions in New Product Development". *Journal of Product Innovation Management* 2, 92-100.

Banerjee S., and Hopp W. J. 2001. "The Project Portfolio Management Problem". Northwestern University Paper.

Banks J. S., and Sundaram R. K. 1994. "Switching Costs and the Gittins Index". *Econometrica* 62 (3), 687-694.

Bass F. M. 1969. "A New-Product Growth Model for Consumer Durables". *Management Science* 15 (1), 215-227.

Bayus B. 1997. "Speed-to-Market and Product Performance Trade-offs". *Journal of Product Innovation Management* 14, 485-497.

Beaujon, G. J., Marin S. P., and McDonald G. C. 2001. "Balancing and optimizing a portfolio of R&D projects". *Naval Logistics Quarterly* 48 (1), 18 - 40.

Beged-Dov A. G. 1965. "Optimal Assignment of R&D Projects in a Large Company Using an Integer Programming Model". *IEEE Transactions on Engineering Management* EM-12, 138-142.

Belhe U. and Kusiak A. 1997. "Dynamic Scheduling of Design Activities with Resource Constraints". *IEEE Transactions on Systems, Man, and Cybernetics* 27 (1), 105-111.

Benson, B., A. S. Sage, and G. Cook. 1993. "Emerging Technology Evaluation Methodology: With Application to Micro-Electromechanical Systems," *IEEE Transactions on Engineering Management* 40 (2), 114-123.

Bertsekas D. 1997. *Dynamic Programming and Optimal Control.* Athena Scientific, Belmont, MA.

Bertsimas D., and Niño-Mora J. 1996. "Conservation Laws, Extended Polymatroids and Multi-Armed Bandit Problems; A Polyhedral Approach to Indexable Systems". *Mathematics of Operations Research* 21 (2), 257-306.

Bertsimas D., and Niño-Mora J. 2000. "Restless Bandits, Linear Programming Relaxations and a Primal-Dual Index Heuristic". *Operations Research* 48 (1), 80-90.

Blackburn J. D. 1991. *Time-Based Competition: The Next Battleground in American Manufacturing.* Business One Irwin.

Boulding W., Ruskin M., and Staelin R. 1997. "Pulling the Plug to Stop the New Product Drain". *Journal of Marketing Research* 34 (1), 164-176.

Braunstein D. M., and Salsamendi M. C. 1994. "R&D Planning at ARCO Chemical". *Research Technology Management*, September-October, 33-47.

Brenner M. S. 1994. "Practical R&D Project Prioritization". *Research Technology Management*, September-October, 38-42.

Brooks, F. P. 1975. *The Mythical Man Month*. Addison Wesley, Reading.

Brucker P., Drexl A., Möhring R., Neumann K., and Pesch E. 1999. "Resource-Constrained Project Scheduling: Notation, Classification, Models and Methods". *European Journal of Operational Research* 112 (1), 3-41.

Cabral-Cardoso C., and Payne R. L. 1996. "Instrumental and Supportive use of Formal Selection Methods in R&D Project Selection". *IEEE Transactions on Engineering Management* 43 (4), 402-410.

Chikte S. 1977. *Markov Decision Models for Optimal Stochastic Resource Allocation Problems*. Unpublished Ph.D. Dissertation. Polytechnic Institute of New York.

Childs P. D., and Triantis A. J. 1999. "Dynamic Investment R&D Policies". *Management Science* 45 (10), 1359-1377.

Clark K. B. 1989. "Project Scope and Project Performance: The Effects of Parts and Supplier Strategy in Product Development". *Management Science* 35 (10), 1247-1263.

Comstock G. L., and Sjolseth D. E. 1999. "Aligning and Prioritizing Corporate R&D". *Research Technology Management*, May-June, 19-25.

Constantinides G. M., and Malliaris A. G. 1995. "Portfolio Theory". R. A. Jarrow, V. Maksimovic, and W. T. Zemba eds. *Handbook in Operations Research and Management Science*. Elsevier Press, Amsterdam, Holland.

Cooper R. G., Edgett S. J., and Kleinschmidt E. J. 1998. *Portfolio Management for New Products*. Perseus Books, New York, NY.

Corbett C. J., and Van Wassenhove L. N. 1993. "The Natural Drift: What Happened to Operations Research?" *Operations Research* 41 (4), 625-640.

Cox D. R., and Smith W. L. 1961. *Queues*. John Wiley. New York.

Czajkowski A. F., and Jones S. 1986. "Selecting Interrelated R&D Projects in Space Technology Planning". *IEEE Transactions on Engineering Management* 33 (1), 624-640.

Cusumano, M. A., and Nobeoka K. 1998. *Thinking Beyond Lean: How Multi-Project Management is Transforming Product Development at Toyota and Others.* The Free Press, New York, NY.

Datar S., Jordan C. C., Kekre S., Rajiv S. and Srinivasan K. 1997. "Advantages of Time-Based New Product Development in a Fast-Cycle Industry". *Journal of Marketing Research* 34 (1), 36-49.

Demeulemeester E. L., and Herroelen W. S. 2002. *Project Scheduling – A Research Handbook*. Kluwer Academic Publishers, Dordrecht.

Ding M., and Eliashberg J. 2002. "Structuring the Product Development Pipeline". *Management Science* 48 (3), 343-363.

Dixit A. K., and R. S. Pindyck. 1994. *Investment Under Uncertainty*. Princeton University Press, Princeton NJ.

Dickinson M. W., Thornton A. C., and Graves S. 2001. "Technology Portfolio Management: Optimizing Interdependent Projects Over Multiple Time Periods". *IEEE Transactions on Engineering Management* 48 (4), 518-527.

Foster T. M. 1996. "Making R&D More Effective at Westinghouse". *Research Technology Management*, January-February, 31-37.

Fox, G. E., Baker N. R., and Bryant J. L. 1984. "Economic Models for R and D Project Selection in the Presence of Project Interactions". *Management Science* 30 (7), 890-904.

Fox G. E., and Baker N. R. 1985. "Project Selection Decision Making Linked to a Dynamic Environment". *Management Science* 31 (10), 1272-1285.

Gittins J. C. 1989. *Multi-armed Bandit Allocation Indices.* John Wiley, New York.

Gittins J. C., and Jones D. M. 1972. "A Dynamic Allocation Index for the Sequential Design of Experiments". *Progress In Statistics: European Meeting of Statisticians.* Budapest: 1972.

Goldratt E. M. 1997. *Critical Chain.* The North River Press, Great Barrington, MA.

Groenveld P. "Roadmapping Integrates Business and Technology". *Research Technology Management,* September-October 1997, 48-55.

Gupta D. K., and Mandakovic T. 1992. "Contemporary Approaches to R&D Project Selection, a Literature Survey". D. F. Kocaogly, (ed.) *Management of R&D and Engineering.* Elsevier Publishers, 67-86.

Ha A. Y. 1997. "Optimal Dynamic Scheduling Policy for a Make to Stock Production System". *Operations Research* 45 (1), 42-53.

Ha A. Y., and Porteus E. L. 1995. "Optimal Timing of Reviews in Concurrent Engineering for Manufacturability". *Management Science* 41 (9), 1431-1447.

Hamel. G. 2000. *Leading the Revolution.* Harvard Business School Press, Boston.

Hamel. G., and Prahalad, C. K. 1989. "Strategic Intent." *Harvard Business Review,* May-June, 2-14.

Hammonds J.S., Keeney R. L., and Raiffa H. 1998. "Even Swaps: A Rational Method for Making Trade-offs". *Harvard Business Review,* March-April, 137-149.

Harrison J. M. 1975. "Dynamic Scheduling of a Multi-class Queue: Discount Optimality". *Operations Research* 23 (2), 270-282.

Hart, S. 1993. "Dimensions of Success in Product Development: an Exploratory Investigation." *Journal of Marketing Management* 9, 23-41.

Hendricks K. B., and Singhal V. R. 1997. "Delays in New Product introductions and the Market Value of the Firm: The Consequences of Being Late to Market". *Management Science* 43 (4), 422-436.

Henriksen A. D., and Traynor A. J. 1999. "A Practical R&D Project-Selection Scoring Tool". *IEEE Transactions on Engineering Management* 46 (2), 158-170.

Hess S. W. 1993. "Swinging on the Branch of a Tree: Project Selection Applications". *Interfaces* 23, (6), 5-12.

House C. H., and Price R. L. 1991. "The Return Map: Tracking Product Teams". *Harvard Business Review* 69 (1), 92-100.

Huchzermeier A., and Loch C. H. 2001. "Project Management Under Risk: Using the Real Options Approach to Evaluate Flexibility in R&D". *Management Science* 47 (1), 85-101.

Ittner C. D., and Larcker D. F. 1997. "Product Development Cycle Time and Organizational Performance". *Journal of Marketing Research* 34 (1), 13-23.

Jones N. 1999. "Competing After Radical Change: The Significance of Product Line Management Strategy". *Working Paper. Ivey School of Business.*

Kaplan, R. S., and Norton D. P. 1996. *The Balanced Scorecard.* Harvard Business School Press, Boston.

Kaplan, R. S., and Norton D. P. 2000. "Having Trouble With Your Strategy – Then Map it." *Harvard Business Review,* September-October, 167-176.

Kavadias S., and Loch C. H. 2003. "Dynamic Prioritization of Projects at a Scarce Resource." *Production and Operations Management* 12(4).

Kavadias S., Loch C. H., and Tapper U. A. S. 2003. "Using Marginal Returns to Allocate the R&D Budget at GemStone". INSEAD Working Paper, August.

Kessler E. H., and Bierly P. E. 2002. "Is Faster Really Better? An Empirical Test of the Implications of Innovation Speed". *IEEE Transactions on Engineering Management* 49 (1), 2-12.

Kleywegt, A. J., and J. D. Papastavrou. 1998. The Dynamic and Stochastic Knapsack Problem. *Operations Research* 46 (1), 17-35.

Kleywegt, A. J., and J. D. Papastavrou. 2001. The Dynamic and Stochastic Knapsack Problem with Random Sized Items. *Operations Research* 49 (1), 26 - 41.

Lewis, M. E., H. Ayhan, R. D. Foley. 1999. Bias Optimality in a Queue With Admission Control. *Probability in the Engineering and Informational Sciences* (13), 309-327.

Liberatore M. J. 1987. "An Extension of the Analytical Hierarchy Process for Industrial R&D Project Selection". *IEEE Transactions on Engineering Management* 34 (1), 12-18.

Liberatore M. J., and Titus G. J. 1983. "The Practice of Management Science in R&D Project Management". *Management Science* 29 (8), 962-974.

Lippman S. A., and S.M. Ross. 1971. "The Streetwalker's Dilemma: A Job Shop Model." *SIAM Journal of Applied Mathematics* 20 (3), 336-342.

Loch C. H. 1996. "American Switching Systems". INSEAD Case Study.

Loch C. H. 1999. "Acer Mobile Systems Unit (A&B)". INSEAD Case Study.

Loch C. H. 2000. "Tailoring Product Development to Strategy: The Case of a European Technology Manufacturer". *European Management Journal* 18 (3), 246-258.

Loch C. H., and Bode-Greuel K. 2001. "Evaluating Growth Options as Sources of Value for Pharmaceutical Research Projects". *R&D Management* 31 (2), 201-248.

Loch C. H., and Huberman B. 1999. "A Punctuated-Equilibrium Model of Technology Diffusion". *Management Science* 45 (2), 160-177.

Loch C. H., and S. Kavadias. 2000. "Gemstone Inc.: Measuring Research Performance". INSEAD Case Study.

Loch C. H., and S. Kavadias. 2002. "Dynamic Portfolio Selection of NPD Programs Using Marginal Returns." *Management Science* 48 (10), 1227-1241.

Loch, C. H., Pich M. T.,Urbschat M., and Terwiesch C. 2001. "Selecting R&D Projects at BMW: A Case Study of Adopting Mathematical Programming Models," *IEEE Transactions on Engineering Management* 48 (1), 70-80.

Loch C. H., and Tapper S. 2002. "Implementing a Strategy-Driven Performance Measurement System for an Applied Research Group". *Journal of Product Innovation Management* 19 (3), 185-198.

Loch C. H., and Terwiesch C. 1999. "Accelerating the Process of Engineering Change Orders". *Journal of Product Innovation Management* 16 (2), 145-159.

Luehrman T. A. 1998. "Investment Opportunities as Real Options: Getting Started With the Numbers". *Harvard Business Review*, July-August, 51-67.

Mahajan S., and Van Ryzin G. 2001. "Stochastic Retail Assortments under Dynamic Consumer Substitution". *Operations Research* 49 (3), 334-351.

Markides, C. C. 1999. "A Dynamic View of Strategy." *Sloan Management Review*, Spring, 55-63.

Meredith J. R. 2001. "Reconsidering the Philosophical Basis of OR/MS". *Operations Research* 49 (3), 325-333.

Merton R. C. 1969. "Lifetime portfolio selection under uncertainty: the continuous-time case". *Review of Economics and Statistics* 51 (8), 247-257.

Meyer M., and Utterback J. M. 1995. "Product Development Cycle Time and Commercial Success". *IEEE Transactions omn Engineering Management* 42 (4), 297-304.

Miller B. L. 1969. "A Queueing Reward System With Several Customer Classes." *Management Science* 16 (3), 234-245.

Nash P. 1980. "A Generalized Bandit Problem". *Journal of the Royal Statistical Society B* 42, 165-169.

Neumann K., Schwindt C., and Zimmermann J. 2002. *Project Scheduling with Time Windows and Scarce Resources*. Springer-Verlag, Berlin.

Newton D. P., and Pearson A. W. 1994. "Application of Option Pricing Theory to R&D". *R&D Management* 24, 83-89.

Nobeoka K., and Cusumano M. A. 1997. "Multiproject Strategy and Sales Growth: The Benefits of Rapid Design Transfer in New Product Development". *Strategic Management Journal* 18 (3), 169-186.

Prastacos G. P. 1981. "Optimal Sequential Investment Decisions Under Conditions of Uncertainty". *Management Science* 29 (1), 118-134.

Reinertsen, D. 1997. *Managing the Design Factory*. The Free Press, New York.

Roberts K, and Weitzman M. L. 1981. "Funding Criteria for Research, Development, and Exploration Projects". *Econometrica* 49 (5), 1261-1288.

Ross, S. M. 1982. *Introduction to Stochastic Dynamic Programming*. John Wiley Press, New York, NY.

Roussel P. A., Saad K. M., and Erickson T. J. 1991. *3rd Generation R&D*. Harvard Business School Press, Boston, MA.

Saaty T. L. 1994. "The Analytic Hierarchy Process". *Interfaces* 24 (6), 19-43.

Samuelson P. A. 1969. "Lifetime Portfolio Selection by Dynamic Stochastic Programming". *Review of Economics and Statistics* 51 (1), 215-227.

Schmidt R. L. 1993. "A Model of R&D Project Selection With COmbined Benefit, Outcome and Resource Interactions". *IEEE Transactions on Engineering Management* 40 (4), 403-410.

Schmidt R. L., and Calantone R. G. 1998. "Are Really New Product Development Projects Harder to Shut Down?". *Journal of Product Innovation Management* 15 (2), 111-123.

Schmidt, R. L., and J. R. Freeland, 1992. "Recent Progress in Modeling R&D Project-Selection Processes," *IEEE Transactions on Engineering Management* 39 (2), 189-199.

Sharpe P., and Kellin T. 1998. "How Smith Kline Beecham Makes Better Resource-Allocation Decisions" *Harvard Business Review* March-April, 45-57.

Smith W. E. 1956. "Various Optimizers for Single-Stage Production". *Naval Research Logistics*. 3, 59-66.

Souder, W. E. 1973. "Analytical Effectiveness of Mathematical Models for R&D Project Selection," *Management Science* 19, 907-923.

Souder, W. E. 1978. "Project Selection, Planning, and Control" in: Moder J. J., and Elmaghraby S. E. (eds.): *Handbook in Operations Research*, New York: Van Nostrand Reinhold.

Stidham, S. 1985. Optimal Control of Admission to a Queueing System. *IEEE Transactions on Automatic Control* AC-30 (8), 705-713.

Stillman H. M. 1997. "How ABB Decides on the Right Technology Investments". *Research Technology Management.* November-December, 14-22.

Stork F. 2000. "Branch-and-Bound Algorithms for Stochastic Resource-Constrained Project Scheduling". Research Report 702/2000, TU Berlin.

Taggart J. H., and Blaxter T. J. 1992. "Strategy in Pharmaceutical R&D: a Portfolio Risk Matrix". *R&D Management.* 22 (3), 241-254.

Terwiesch, C., C. H. Loch. 1999. "Measuring the Effectiveness of Overlapping Development Activities." *Management Science* 45 (4), 455-465.

Tritle G. L., Seriven E. F. V., and Fusfeld A. R. 2000. "Resolving Uncertainty in R&D Portfolios". *Research Technology Management.* November-December, 47-55.

Trigeorgis L. 1996. *Real Options: Managerial Flexibility and Strategy in Resource Allocation.* The MIT Press. Cambridge Massachusetts.

Ulrich K., and Eppinger S. D. 2003. *Product Design and Development.* 3rd Edition. Irwin-McGraw Hill, New York, NY.

Van Mieghem J. 1995. "Dynamic Scheduling with Convex Delay Costs: The Generalized $c\mu$ Rule". *The Annals of Applied Probability* 5 (3), 808-833.

Van Mieghem J. 2000. "Price and Service Discrimination in Queueing Systems: Incentive-Compatible G-$c\mu$ Rules". *Management Science* 46 (9), 1249-1267.

Van Mieghem J. 2001. "Due-Date Scheduling: Asymptotic Optimality of Generalized Longest Queue and Generalized Largest Delay Rules". *Operations Research* 51 (1), 113-122.

Van Oyen M. P., Pandelis D. G., and Teneketzis D. 1992. "Optimality of Index Policies for Stochastic Scheduling With Switching Penalties". *Journal of Applied Probability* 29, 957-966.

Veatch M., and Wein L. 1996. "Scheduling of a Make-to-Stock Queue: Indexing Policies and Hedging Points". *Operations Research* 44 (4), 634-647.

Vishwanath T. 1992. "Optimal Orderings for Parallel Project Selection". *International Economic Review* 33 (1), 79-89.

Weber R. R., and Weiss G. 1990. "On an Index Policy for Restless Bandits". *Journal of Applied Probability.* 27, 637-648.

Wein L. 1992. "Dynamic Scheduling of a Multiclass Make-to-Stock Queue". *Operations Research.* 40 (4), 724-735.

Weitzman M. L. 1979. "Optimal Search for the Best Alternative". *Econometrica* 47 (3), 641-654.

Wheelwright S. C., and Clark K. B. 1992a. *Revolutionizing New Product Development.* The Free Press, New York, NY.

Wheelwright S. C., and Clark K. B. 1992b. "Creating ProjectPlans to Focus Product Development." *Harvard Business Review*, March-April, 70-82.

Whittle P. 1980. "Multi-Armed Bandits and the Gittins' Index". *Journal of Royal Statistical Society* 42 (2), 143-149.

Whittle P. 1988. "Restless Bandits: Activity Allocation in A Changing World". *Journal of Applied Probability* 25A, 287-298.

Williamson P. 1999. "Strategy as Options on the Future". *Sloan Management Review*, Spring, 117-126.

About the Authors

Stylianos (Stelios) Kavadias is Assistant Professor at the Dupree College of Management of the Georgia Institute of Technology (Georgia Tech). His research focuses on project selection, competition effects in new product development, and the management of the product development process and of new technologies.

Stelios Kavadias was awarded 2nd place in the 2001 *Dantzig Best Dissertation Competition* of the INFORMS Society for his doctoral thesis work on portfolio selection in new product development. An evolution of this research is presented in this book. He has published his work in *Management Science* and *Production and Operations Management*, and he is on the editorial review board of *Production and Operations Management*. He is currently teaching the new product development and management of technology MBA courses at Georgia Tech, as well as a Ph.D. course on Technology Management.

Stelios Kavadias holds a Ph.D. degree in Management from INSEAD, an MS in Management from INSEAD, and a Diploma (MS equivalent) in Electrical and Computer Engineering from the National Technical University of Athens (NTUA).

Christoph H. Loch is Professor of Technology Management at INSEAD. His research revolves around the management of R&D and the product innovation process, particularly technology strategy, project selection, concurrent engineering, project management under high uncertainty, collaborative problem solving, and performance measurement. He is also interested in the effects of status competition, and its interaction with culture, in organizations.

Christoph Loch is associate editor of *Management Science* and *Operations Research*, department editor for *Production and Operations Management*, and a senior editor of *Manufacturing & Service Operations Management*. His work has appeared in *Management Science, Organization Science, Social Psychology Quarterly*, the *Journal of Product Innovation Management, R&D Management, IEEE Transaction on Engineering Management*, the *Journal of Organizational Computing*, the *Journal of Economic Behavior & Organization, Concurrent Engineering Research and Applications*, the *International Journal of Project Management, Sloan Management Review, European Management Journal*, and the *Financial Times*. He has also co-authored one book on management quality in manufacturing and written several chapters in books on innovation management. He teaches MBA, executive and Ph.D. courses at INSEAD, consults on technology management, and serves on the supervisory board of an educational software start-up company.

Christoph Loch holds a Ph.D. in business from the Graduate School of Business at Stanford University, an MBA from the University of Tennessee in Knoxville, and a Diplom-Wirtschaftsingenieur degree from the Darmstadt Institute of Technology in Germany. Prior to joining IN-SEAD, he worked as a consultant for McKinsey & Company in their San Francisco and Munich offices.

Index

Early Titles in the
INTERNATIONAL SERIES IN
OPERATIONS RESEARCH & MANAGEMENT SCIENCE
Frederick S. Hillier, Series Editor, *Stanford University*

***A list of the more recent publications in the series is at the front of the book ***